Performance CARS

Performance
CARS

Jonathan Wood

PARRAGON

First published in 1999 by Parragon

Parragon
Queen Street House
4 Queen Street
Bath BA1 1HE
United Kingdom

Designed, produced and packaged by
Stonecastle Graphics Limited
Old Chapel Studio, Plain Road, Marden
Tonbridge, Kent TN12 9LS United Kingdom

ISBN 0-75253-154-9

Printed in Italy

Photographic Credits:

Neill Bruce: pages 2, 7, 9, 12 (*top*), 14, 15, 18-19 (*top*), 19 (*below*), 22, 23, 26 (*top*), 28-29, 30 (*below*), 31, 32 (*top*), 33, 38 (*top*), 41 (*right*), 46, 47 (*top*), 50 (*top*), 52, 53, 54 (*top*), 55, 58, 59, 68, 72 (*top*), 74, 75, 77, 78, 79, 84, 85 (*below*), 86, 87, 95 (*below*).

All other photographs are from the Peter Roberts Collection of manufacturers' press pictures, c/o Neill Bruce.

CONTENTS

FRANCE: CLEVER BUT CONSTRAINED

Currently Renault and Peugeot/Citroën, as France's Big Two motor manufacturers, concentrate their energies on satisfying the needs of the highly competitive mass market. Performance cars tend to be variants of popular models although, as will emerge, the growth in recent years of low volume niche vehicles continues to produce some pleasant surprises!

IT HAS not always been so. France is the country that in pre-war days gave the world the large-engined, high-speed Bugattis, Delahayes and Lago-Talbots.

One of the principal reasons for the current dearth of such exotic machinery is taxation. Since the early post-war years owners of cars of over 7CV (horsepower), the equivalent of an engine capacity of about 3 litres, have been penalized by a swingeing annual tax rate.

With little incentive for manufacturers to produce large capacity, and thus ultra-fast, elegant grand tourers, with a few notable exceptions the breed has all but disappeared. And those car makers which have offered such models invariably stayed the right side of the important 3-litre ceiling.

One of the more memorable examples is Citroën's Franco/Italian hybrid, a fearsomely complex Maserati-engined SM of 1970–75, a car soon cancelled by Peugeot which bought Citroën in 1974 and is still custodian of the make.

Back in 1912 Peugeot invented the high performance, twin-overhead-camshaft engine, a configuration that powers practically all performance cars currently in production.

For a time Peugeot also owned Matra before selling it to Renault. The Matra car is no longer built and the factory at Romorantin now produces the Renault Espace people carrier, which is also manufactured in Dieppe.

Also built there is Renault's ingenious and idiosyncratic low-volume, mid-engined Sport Spider. This factory was once the home of the Alpine sports car, one of France's most successful performance models, although this producer of the small Renault-

based rear-engined coupes and roadsters was bought by the state-owned car giant in 1974.

An Alpine-Renault won the Le Mans 24 hour race in 1978 and Matra also has the distinction of being the French make to have triumphed in the event on the most occasions. It took the chequered flag in three successive years between 1972 and 1974.

The world's most famous motoring competition has been an integral part of the French racing calendar since its 1923 inception and ever since it has provided an irresistible lure to car makers old and new, at home or abroad.

The race has always attracted ambitious, small, vulnerable, but publicity-conscious producers of performance models. One such was the Nantes-built Venturi, but the financial demands of the event in the 1990s proved to be its undoing.

Happily, this interesting French grand tourer was saved and it continues in production under new ownership. Power comes from Renault's ubiquitous V6 saloon car engine, but it should be remembered that France's largest motor manufacturer also has an enviable reputation as a producer of Formula 1 power units.

These engines have been employed by every world championship-winning Formula 1 team from 1992 until 1997, a less apparent but nonetheless potent reminder of the versatility of one of Europe's most successful motor industries.

Above: Last of a line, the spirit of the pre-war French high-speed coupes lived on in the 2.5 litre Talbot-Lago America of 1955. It was built until 1960.

Left: The Dieppe-made rear-engined 130mph (209km/h) Alpine-Renault 310 V6, introduced in 1971, was powered by Renault's 2.6 V6 engine from 1977 until 1985.

Right: Now in abeyance, Matra began building cars in 1965. This is the steel-bodied Murena of 1980 with 2.2 litre Chrysler power. Earlier cars were glass fibre.

Peugeot 206 GTi

One of the early hot hatchbacks, Peugeot's GTi provided its best-selling 205 – over five million were sold world-wide – with a much-needed boost, and this hotted-up variant is being perpetuated with its 206 successor.

WITH STUNNING styling by Peugeot's own design studio, rather than Pininfarina who were responsible for its predecessor's acclaimed lines, the hatchback is available in three- and five-door forms.

Peugeot unveiled the 206 in mid-1998, and the GTi version at the 1998 Paris Motor Show. This go-faster model went on sale in 1999. Produced, like its predecessor, in two-door form only, the GTi is externally identifiable by its slightly flared front wings, low-mounted driving lamps and 15-inch five-spoked alloy wheels. The door handles, wing mirrors and number plate mountings are all colour keyed.

Beneath the bonnet, this hot 206 is the first recipient of a brand new 2 litre Peugeot engine, internally coded EW10J4, an all-aluminium, twin-overhead-camshaft four developing a spirited 138bhp, which compares with the 110bhp of the top-line 16-valve 1.6. This new power unit will also be extended, in enlarged forms, to Peugeot's 306 hatchback and 406 saloon range.

From the front the Peugeot 206GTi clearly means business with flared wheel arches and low-mounted driving lamps.

SPECIFICATION	PEUGEOT 206 GTi
Engine location	Front, transverse
Configuration	4-cylinder
Bore and stroke	85 x 88mm
Capacity	1997cc
Valve operation	Twin overhead camshaft, 4 valves per cylinder
Horsepower	137bhp @ 6000rpm
Transmission	Five speed
Drive	Front
Chassis	Unitary
Suspension – front	MacPherson strut
Suspension – rear	Trailing arm
Brakes	Disc, ventilated at front
Top speed	130mph (209km/h)
Acceleration	0-100mph (0-161km/h) 8.4 seconds

It is mounted in a more upright position than earlier power units in the engine bay; less apparent are the lightweight timing gears intended to reduce internal friction. An alloy sump cover is also a feature. The aluminium theme is echoed inside the car with an alloy gearlever knob and pedals. There are leather-trimmed seats and steering wheel, and air conditioning is fitted.

Top speed is 130mph (209km/h) and this hot Gallic hatchback, which is to be known as the 206 S16 in its homeland, can cover a standing kilometre in less than 30 seconds. Its 205 GTi predecessor enjoyed a 10-year production life, the 206 has got off to a similarly successful start.

Peugeot is also producing a Rally version of the 206 which bristles with such goodies as a 300bhp 2 litre turbocharged engine, six-speed gearbox and four-wheel-drive. The company won the world rally championship with the 205 in 1985.

Renault sport Spider

Renault's quirky fun car not only offers potential buyers the roadholding of a racer, it is also similarly devoid of such creature comforts as a windscreen, side windows or even door locks!

Spiders sold on the UK market are fitted with a windscreen!

CONCEIVED ON a Spring day in 1993 by Renault's head of styling, Patrick le Quement, and the company's director of motorsport, Christian Contzen, it was intended as a spiritual successor to the no-frills Lotus Seven.

It was announced just two years later, in March 1995, and coincidentally just four months later Lotus unveiled its latter-day Seven in the form of the mid-engined Elise (see pages 72–73) built up around an extruded aluminium chassis.

This material is also at the Sport's heart in the form of an aluminium space-frame which makes a significant contribution to the car weighing a mere 1740lb (790kg). Renault claimed that it was some 40 per cent lighter than a similar steel counterpart.

The mid-located power unit is a 2 litre, twin-overhead-camshaft, four-valve per cylinder engine, with iron block and alloy head, courtesy of the Clio Williams. Developing 150bhp, it drives the rear wheel via a five-speed gearbox.

But the most daring aspect of the two-seater design is its uncompromising styling. With polyester composite yellow panels juxtaposed with contrasting black, the Sport was created, like the trans-Atlantic Beach Buggy, for sunny climes. Accordingly there is no windscreen. Windows were regarded as unnecessary and functionality reigned supreme, with the car's chunky lines only being interrupted by a protective rollover bar.

The all-round double wishbones with racing-type rose joints are courtesy of Renault's discontinued A610. The ventilated disc brakes from the same source provide the stopping power.

It comes as no surprise to find that the Sport Spider is produced at the former Alpine factory in Dieppe. Production of these classic Renault-based sports cars began there as long ago as 1965.

Bearing this in mind, the original idea was to accord the Spider the Alpine name. Unfortunately that is owned, in Britain at least, by Renault's Peugeot rival!

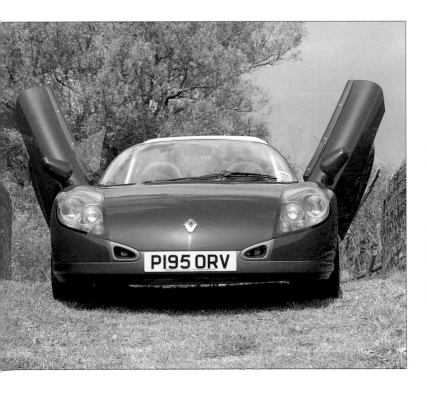

SPECIFICATION	RENAULT SPORT SPIDER
Engine location	Mid, longitudinal
Configuration	4-cylinder
Bore and stroke	82 x 93mm
Capacity	1998cc
Valve operation	Twin overhead camshaft, 4 valves per cylinder
Horsepower	150bhp @ 6000rpm
Transmission	Five speed
Drive	Rear
Chassis	Aluminium space-frame
Suspension – front	Wishbones and coil springs
Suspension – rear	Wishbones and coil springs
Brakes	Ventilated disc
Top speed	130mph (209km/h)
Acceleration	0-60mph (0-97km/h) 7 seconds

Unorthodoxy extends to the doors which swivel upwards in supercar style. There are no windows, only quarter lights.

Renault sport Clio V6 24V

One of a handful of so-called superhatches, a 150mph (241km/h) mid-engined version of Renault's best-selling Clio hatchback made a surprise appearance at the 1998 Paris Motor Show. Endowed with a 3 litre V6 engine, the Renault sport Trophy entered production in 1999.

THE ORIGINAL front-wheel-drive Clio supermini, a lively and chic hatchback, was the first of a family of Renaults to be identified by a name rather than a number. With over three million built, it was replaced in 1998 as Europe's best-selling French car by the Clio II with engines ranging in size from 1.2 to 1.9 litres.

But unlike the original, the second generation model is offered with a mid-located, 3 litre, twin-overhead-camshaft, 24-valve V6, derived from the engine used in Renault's Laguna saloon. Uprated from 190bhp to develop 250, it is transversely located, intrudes into the car and occupies the passenger space hitherto taken up by the rear seat. It thus drives the rear, as opposed to the front wheels via a specially developed five speed gearbox.

Although the substructure is based on a modified Clio floorpan, complete with revised longirons and crossmembers, special outer panels are made of weight-saving composite panels.

Outwardly this Clio is something special, even though the bodyshell, bonnet, rear hatch and roof are production components. But the doors are profiled to accommodate the engine's air intakes and there are extended wheel arches to cater for the special 17-inch wheels with low-profile tyres tailored for the race track. Substantial cross-ventilated all-round disc brakes ensures that this potent hatchback stop as well as it goes.

The model has been deliberately conceived to evoke memories of the fearsome competition-honed Renault 5 Turbo 2, a homologation special built in 1983–1986.

This latter-day rendition has a dual personality. It has been developed by Renault sport and the Trophy version is to be run in special Clio Renault sport Trophy events to support rounds of Formula 1 and British Touring Car Championship events.

The other is a road-goer that appeared some six months after the racers broke cover. But these potent V6-powered hatchbacks

Above: The V6's dashboard is from the top-of-the-range Clio, but with a 170mph (280km/h) speedometer and additional white-faced instruments. The trim and upholstery are leather and Alcantara.

Left: You're never far away from the potent V6, derived from the Laguna saloon engine.

Above: The alloy and composite bodywork keeps the weight down to 2645lb (1200kg).

possess refinements a world away from their track-prepared first cousins. They feature air conditioning, power steering and electric windows, as well as leather and suede upholstery.

The dashboard is related to the mainstream Clios and the brushed aluminium gearlever surrounds and door trimmings are suggestive of the Audi TT. However, interior luggage space is limited to the small area behind the front seats and the engine.

If you should encounter what appears to be a standard Clio at the traffic lights, but one graced with a pair of discreet Renault sport badges on its tailgate, don't be surprised if it goes off like a rocket. A 0 to 60mph (97km/h) figure of 5.5 seconds is claimed...

SPECIFICATION	RENAULT SPORT CLIO V6 24V
Engine location	Mid, transverse
Configuration	V6
Bore and stroke	87 x 82mm
Capacity	2946cc
Valve operation	Twin overhead camshafts, 4 valves per cylinder
Horsepower	250bhp @ 6500rpm
Transmission	Five speed
Drive	Rear
Chassis	Unitary
Suspension – front	MacPherson strut
Suspension – rear	MacPherson strut/trailing arm
Brakes	Ventilated disc
Top speed	150mph (241km/h)
Acceleration	0-60mph (0-97km/h) 5.5 seconds

Venturi Atlantique 300

The name may sound unfamiliar but this luxurious mid-engined Venturi coupe, with a top speed of 174mph (280km/h), is France's fastest production car.

IT WAS back in 1984 that Claude Poiraud and Gerald Godfroy applied their experiences of long-distance sports car racing to launch the Venturi concept at the 1984 Paris Motor Show.

By 1986 a turbocharged four-cylinder-powered prototype had appeared but the two production versions, the 2.4 litre 210 coupe and cabriolet and 2.8 litre 260 coupe, that entered production in 1987, were both turbocharged and powered by Renault's well-proven V6 engine.

In 1989, Primwest, a financial services company, became Venturi's backer and in the following year a new factory was established at Nantes. The firm even built its own race track and customers were able to test-drive their cars on delivery.

Soon afterwards, in 1992, came the Gentleman Drivers Trophy intended for Venturi owners. It was staged at important international race meetings and the factory produced a new design for enthusiastic amateurs to campaign in these events.

This was the 400GT, longer and wider than the old cars with a distinctive rear spoiler. It visually owed much to Ferrari's celebrated F40. A batch of 16 were built in this introductory year.

Top: The Venturi is particularly well appointed even if the dashboard layout is a little dated. Leather is used to good effect and the seats offer excellent support.

SPECIFICATION	VENTURI ATLANTIQUE 300
Engine location	Mid, longitudinal
Configuration	V6, twin turbocharged
Bore and stroke	87 x 87mm
Capacity	2975cc
Valve operation	Twin overhead camshafts, 4 valves per cylinder
Horsepower	302bhp @ 5500rpm
Transmission	Five speed
Drive	Rear
Chassis	Unitary
Suspension – front	Wishbone and coil springs
Suspension – rear	Trailing arm
Brakes	Ventilated disc
Top speed	174mph (280km/h)
Acceleration	0-60mph (0-97km/h) 5.3 seconds

Above: The V6 Renault-engined 300 with composite body. Its location is indicated by the air intakes above the back wheels. Beneath is a steel chassis. Automatic transmission arrived for 1999.

Right: Externally identical to the automatic, the 1999 range was marked by the arrival of twin turbochargers. Right-hand-drive versions are rare. UK sales are aimed at 25 cars a year.

Power came from a twin turbocharged 3 litre version of the ubiquitous Renault six. In this form it developed 408bhp, hence the model's designation.

After two years of races, in 1994 Venturi introduced a roadgoing version – a notable feature was the brakes, as the company claimed that the 400 was the first production car in the world to be fitted with carbon-fibre discs.

Alas, as is often the way with such businesses, Venturi made the mistake of devoting too much of its resources to motor sport, particularly at Le Mans when in 1993–95 it entered eight competitions and finished six times. The 600 GT was developed for the 24 hour classic event, but the road car programme suffered and, as a result, in 1995 the company went out of business.

However, Venturi was revived in 1996 by Thai business interests, and the following year road cars went on sale in Europe. That year the top of range Atlantique 300 was unveiled. It was developed from the earlier cars although every body panel was reworked. Power is still courtesy of Renault's proven alloy 3 litre V6, longitudinally located, although the single Garrett turbocharger was replaced by twin turbos for the 1999 season. As a result power rose by seven per cent, to 302bhp.

Also available is an unblown 210bhp version with manual transmission, although an automatic option is a second 1999 arrival. Its top speed is accordingly somewhat less than the twin turbo, namely 150mph (241km/h) with 60mph (97km/h) arriving in 7.5 seconds, which compares with the 5.3 seconds achieved by its twin turbo stablemate.

The 300 is a well-appointed two-seater with plenty of leather in evidence, and this even applies to the roof lining! Priced in Britain at £60,000, the Atlantique 300 offers fast, distinctive motoring. But it is up against formidable opposition from the likes of the Aston Martin DB7, Jaguar XK8 and TVR Cerbera.

GERMANY: ENGINEERING FOR THE WORLD

 *As the automobile was born in Germany in 1886, it is not surprising to find that the country's motor manufacturers have been producing performance cars for longer than any of the world's other car makers.*

THE OLDEST of them, Mercedes-Benz, with its origins rooted in the two companies that gave birth to the motor car, remains a leading manufacturer of models for both road and track.

Not only does it produce an outstanding range of passenger cars, the Stuttgart company has engineered such epitomes of excellence as the refined and costly SL and fearsome sports-racing CLK-GTR coupe. The latter also forms the basis of a wild, impractical and costly road car.

Like Mercedes-Benz, BMW has gained a worldwide reputation for the excellence of its passenger models, but it also has a long-standing commitment to the performance sector. Its legendary pre-war 328 open two-seater of 1936–40 vintage set a bench mark for sports car design the world over.

This momentum is maintained by the deceptive but potent M-enhanced saloons, while the relatively inexpensive American-built Z3 open two-seater has opened a new and successful market sector for the company. Its M Coupe derivative, however, belongs more in BMW's traditional marketplace.

The Munich-based company has been making cars since 1928. By contrast, Porsche, as one of the world's greatest sports car manufacturers, is a relatively newcomer, not having produced its first car until 1948. This original air-cooled rear-engined 356 coupe was followed in 1963 by the similarly configured 911. That, incredibly, is still in production, 36 years after it first appeared.

Although for a time in the late 1970s and 1980s, Porsche switched the emphasis of its manufacturing philosophy to

conventionally engined grand tourers. They caused a downturn in the company's affairs but the last of these disappeared in 1995.

The company, like Mercedes-Benz, is Stuttgart-based, and is now doing what it does best: namely producing its utterly distinctive rear- and mid-engined sports cars. The latest of these, the two-seater Boxster, appeared in 1996 and this and the 911 form the backbone of the make's increasingly popular two model line.

But there is much more to Porsche than road cars for the marque has won the Le Mans 24 hour race on a record 16 occasions. Its first victory came in 1970 with the magnificent and monumental 917 sports racer, a car conceived by founder Ferdinand Porsche's grandson, Ferdinand Piech, who now heads the Volkswagen group.

The original VW Beetle, the German People's Car, was designed by Porsche in 1934–38 and it is difficult to think of a less sporting car than this original low-cost saloon powered by a noisy air-cooled, rear-mounted, horizontally opposed engine.

This is, nevertheless, why the Porsche company was so committed to this unlikely mechanical configuration and, incredibly, the original Beetle remains in production at VW's Mexican factory.

But with the Volkswagen and its highly successful Golf range still committed to the high-volume sector, the group's performance image has been assiduously honed by Audi, most recently with its acclaimed TT coupe and cabriolet.

And with Volkswagen having, in 1998, bought both the exclusive Lamborghini and Bugatti makes, the uncertainly that clouded the history of both companies is now behind them. Things can only get better.

Above: Mercedes-Benz performance from another era, a 1957 300SL. Powered by a 3 litre, overhead-camshaft, six-cylinder engine, it was capable of 138mph (222km/h).

Left: A brace of superlative German sports cars, a BMW 328 (left) and 1955 Porsche 356 Speedster, when owned by British rally stalwart Betty Haig.

Right: Purity of a long-running line: this 1967 Porsche 911S, identifiable by its alloy wheels, was also owned by Betty Haig.

Audi TT

It started life as a concept car, but this unconventional-looking Audi is the latest adventurous product of the expanding and up-beat Volkswagen empire.

Guaranteed to turn heads, the newly introduced TT skilfully combines old and new themes.

CHUNKY STYLING with one set of its wheels apparently planted in the 1930s and the other two accelerating forward into the 21st century, the TT is based on the same platform as the in-house Golf. It is clearly aimed at the market enjoyed by the likes of the similarly distinctive Porsche Boxster.

The TT is available with a choice of transversely mounted turbocharged engines and drive lines. There is a 180bhp version of Volkswagen's versatile 1.8 litre, four-cylinder, twin-cam, five-valve-per-cylinder engine. This is only slightly more powerful than the unit used in the A3 hatchback. A five-speed gearbox is employed and, in the long-established Audi traditions, it drives the front wheels. Top speed is a respectable 140mph (225km/h).

However, there is an alternative four-wheel-drive Quattro version and a top line TT powered by uprated 225bhp engine both of which use an electro-hydraulic distribution system. This is a good 10mph (16km/h) faster than the base version, being capable of 151mph (243km/h).

A six-speed gearbox is employed and the broad six-spoked alloy wheels echo those made popular by Bugatti of the 1920s.

The TT cabriolet will appear after the coupe, with UK sales scheduled for the year 2000. It also will be available in front- or four-wheel-drive forms.

SPECIFICATION	AUDI TT COUPE
Engine location	Front, transverse
Configuration	4-cylinder turbocharged
Bore and stroke	81 x 86mm
Capacity	1781cc
Valve operation	Twin overhead camshafts, 5 valves per cylinder
Horsepower	225bhp @ 5900rpm
Transmission	Six speed
Drive	Four-wheel
Chassis	Unitary
Suspension – front	MacPherson strut
Suspension – rear	Double wishbones
Brakes	Ventilated disc
Top speed	151mph (243km/h)
Acceleration	0-60mph (0-97km/h) 6.2 seconds

The TT's interior is as unconventional as its bodywork, with black leather trim and brushed aluminium finish; the stereo radio is even concealed behind such a cover. The metal also features on the stubby gearlever and its presence imbues the cockpit with an atmosphere curiously redolent of Zeppelin airship interiors of the 1930s. The same metallic theme is echoed by the racing-style external petrol filler cap.

Highly acclaimed by commentators, the coupe is to be joined by an open cabriolet version for the 2000 season.

Paradoxically the ultra-Germanic TT is not built in that country, but in a new plant that Volkswagen has established in Hungary. It plans to produce some 40,000 of these Audis a year, with a 75/25 per cent allocation in favour of the closed version. Their presences can only enliven the highways of the world.

BMW M5

In BMW parlance M stands for Motorsport and the prefix indicates that this is a rather special version of the company's acclaimed 5 Series saloon.

Although outwardly resembling the mainstream Series 5, wider chrome radiator surrounds and oval fog lights are give-aways.

THE MUNICH-based firm set up its Motorsport division in 1972 and sales of mostly specially modified production models over the past two decades have amounted to 100,000 cars.

The 5 Series dates back to 1972, but the latest example appeared in 1995 and it was offered with a range of six-cylinder engines from 2 litres capacity, followed in 1996 by a top-line 4.4 litre V8. Top speed was 155mph (249km/h).

This third-generation M5 was announced at the 1997 Frankfurt Motor Show, and it uses that engine as its starting point. The 4.9 litre, 32-valve V8 employing twin overhead camshafts per cylinder bank, develops 400bhp.

It incorporates BMW's double Vanox valve-timing system which is applied to both camshafts and has the effect of introducing torque at a lower rev level, while also maintaining it at the all-important top end.

Smooth gas flow is ensured by the presence of separate butterfly valves on each cylinder bank which produces instantaneous responses. A six-speed gearbox, courtesy of the smaller M3, but strengthened to cope with the extra power, is employed.

A 0-60mph (97km/h) figure of just 5.4 seconds means that the M5 is the fastest-accelerating BMW road car ever. It has a top speed of 155mph (249km/h) but this is electronically restricted. Allowed to let rip, it could reach 186mph (300km/h).

Naturally there are the essential modifications to the suspension and brakes, but outwardly the changes are discreet. This

is a real wolf in German sheep dog's clothing. At the front is an enlarged spoiler and new headlamp clusters. Side-on give-aways are modest skirts and sports-type wing mirrors.

At the rear are four, as opposed to the usual two, exhaust pipes and, of course, the M5 badge on the boot lid. Rumour has it that this potent floorpan will form the basis of a Z7 coupe and roadster that could be part of the BMW programme for the year 2000. Worth waiting for!

SPECIFICATION	BMW M5
Engine location	Front, in-line
Configuration	V8
Bore and stroke	94 x 89mm
Capacity	4941cc
Valve operation	Twin overhead camshafts, 4 valves per cylinder
Horsepower	400bhp @ 6600rpm
Transmission	Six speed
Drive	Rear
Chassis	Unitary
Suspension – front	MacPherson strut
Suspension – rear	Multi-link
Brakes	Ventilated disc
Top speed	155mph (249km/h)
Acceleration	0-60mph (0-97km/h) 5.4 seconds

Doing what it does best: an M5 at speed. The handsome chrome-finished wheels that almost fill the entire arches, streamlined mirrors and side skirts are further subtle differences that distinguish it from the mainsteam car. A small aerofoil is fitted to the boot lid.

BMW Z3

In its original 1996 form, the Z3, produced by BMW at its Spartanburg factory in the United States, combined the refinement of the company's finely engineered saloon cars with the performance associated with an open two-seater. But since then the model's engine range has expanded and the roadster has been joined by a purposeful coupe.

Based on the popular Series 3 Compact, the American-built Z3 roadster is available with a choice of 1.8 and 1.9 four-cylinder engines and a 2.8 litre six.

TO DATE well over 100,000 have been built. Certainly the relatively inexpensive Z3 got a rousing send-off because it was used by secret agent James Bond, in place of his more traditional Aston Martin or Lotus, in the film *GoldenEye*, released at the end of 1995.

Although South Carolina-built, the Z3 was engineered by BMW in Germany and is based on the floorpan of the Series 3 Compact sporting hatchback. It was initially powered by a choice of that model's four-cylinder engines.

This meant a 1.8 litre, eight-valve, 115bhp unit while a more exciting 140bhp, 1.9 litre, 16-valve, twin-cam version endowed the roadster with a top speed of 128mph (206km/h) and a 0-62mph (100km/h) time of 9.5 seconds.

The fours were joined for the 1997 season by an alternative 2.8 litre six-cylinder engine, courtesy of BMW's 3, 5 and 7 Series saloons. External changes to the Z3 were minimal, with slightly wider wheel arches, a larger air intake and deeper front air dam. The six made a significant difference to the roadster's performance and resulted in a top speed of 135mph (217km/h).

This was followed by the even-faster Z3 M Roadster, announced in 1996 although deliveries did not begin until the following year. It was powered by the formidable 321bhp 24-valve six used in the M3 and M Roadster and its attendant five-speed manual gearbox. Top speed was 155mph (249km/h).

However, it differs visually from the earlier version because its body has been lowered by 0.4in (10mm), fitted with new bumpers front and rear and a large frontal airdam. By contrast, the four large-diameter stainless steel tailpipes aren't truly functional but generate a rousing symphony for the driver!

SPECIFICATION	BMW Z3 M COUPE
Engine location	Front, in-line
Configuration	6-cylinder
Bore and stroke	86 x 91mm
Capacity	3201cc
Valve operation	Twin overhead camshafts, 4 valves per cylinder
Horsepower	321bhp @ 7400rpm
Transmission	Five speed
Drive	Rear
Chassis	Unitary
Suspension – front	MacPherson Strut
Suspension – rear	Semi-trailing arm
Brakes	Ventilated disc
Top speed	154mph (248km/h)
Acceleration	0-60mph (0-97km/h) 5.2 seconds

Demand for the entire Z3 family caught BMW by surprise and, as a result, it did not manage to produce right-hand-drive versions for the British and Japanese markets until 1997.

This configuration was also extended, in 1998, to a coupe version of the Z3 M Roadster, complete with opening tailgate, that

joined the drophead cars in 1997. The Z3 M coupe is thus only available with the raucous 321bhp six and associated five-speed gearbox; there wasn't room for BMW's latest six cog unit.

Initiated as a private venture by BMW engineers, the conversion, undertaken by a five-man team, took place in an underground garage in the company's research and development centre. This explains its no-nonsense, purposeful appearance although in due course the services of a single stylist were retained.

No attempt was made to extend the wheelbase, so the Z3 coupe remains an uncompromising two-seater although there is rather more luggage space compared to the roadster.

Capable of over 150mph (241km/h), the M coupe is the latest version of the Z3 line, and its rigid structure is regarded by commentators as being a great improvement over the roadster on which it is based. Having said that, the open car has rather more visual appeal. But whatever your tastes, there's clearly plenty of mileage left in the entire Z3 family.

Top inset: The fast and chunky M coupe. It is a hatchback and has considerably more luggage space than the roadster.

Below: The 321bhp six-cylinder engine possesses a split personality, docile in traffic yet formidable and raucous when the need arises.

Mercedes-Benz CLK-GTR

It must be one of the most sensational supercars of all time. The CLK-GTR of 1998 is a roadgoing version of 1997's GT Championship winner and just 25 examples have been built, to sell at £1.1 million apiece. As such, it is the world's most expensive road car.

A racer for the road, the CLK-GTR, mid-engined, wildly impractical but awe-inspiring in appearance and mechanicals, capable of nearly 200mph (322km/h).

LOW, SILVER and sleek, the car sports a miniaturized but very identifiable version of the famous Mercedes–Benz radiator grille and tri-star mascot. These, together with the distinctive recessed head and spotlamps, combine to display an all-important family relationship with the CLK road cars. However, the only shared external component is the rear light cluster!

But this is where the resemblance ends because the remainder of the coupe body and its mechanicals follow the layout of the all-conquering track cars.

The 6.9 litre V12 engine, longitudinally located in the mid position and driving the rear wheels, is bolted directly to the monocoque carbon-fibre hull. The 48-valve 60-degree unit with

iron block and alloy cylinder heads, is based on the corporate 6 litre unit, stroked to 6898cc. It only differs from the track cars in being fitted with tamer camshafts and a reworked engine management system. The outcome is a still astounding 612bhp.

The purposeful reinforced Kevlar body, complete with scissor doors, is finished in obligatory silver. There is a huge rear wing, complete with brake light, to help keep the GTR's massive rear wheels on the road.

Further roadgoing refinements include revised rear suspension to raise the ride height, and a special interior with new sports seating which limits space somewhat. Legislation requires that the engine is fitted with twin closed three-way catalytic converters which are part of the gargantuan exhaust system.

Performance is, not surprisingly, phenomenal with 62mph (100km/h) arriving in just 3.8 seconds. Mercedes-Benz road cars are usually limited to a top speed of 155mph (249km/h) but this silver-hued projectile will hurtle to 199mph (320km/h). The speedometer reads to 340km/h (211mph), but otherwise the instrumentation is courtesy of the CLK.

A competition-bred six-speed Xtrac gearbox is employed with changes effected, racing style, by small paddles positioned behind the steering wheel that turn with it. Perversely the racing version used a manual gear lever and there are suspicions that the lack of interior room in the road car may have rendered this unusable.

Perhaps for this reason, each cockpit is individually tailored for its millionaire owner. Visibility is also something of a luxury because the rear halves of the side windows are false and there is no back one. For this reason, there's no rear-view mirror.

And this not the car in which to do the shopping on a Saturday, even though it is fitted with power steering and brakes, both items being absent from the racing version. Not only is the engine not at its happiest idling at traffic lights, its noisy presence is a constant reminder that it's only inches away behind your head. Fuel consumption is around 8.9mpg (32lit/100km). So forget impressing the neighbours, the GTR is far happier on the race track for which it was built.

And if you're interested in buying a CLK-GTR, forget it. The entire batch has already been sold.

Left: The huge rear wing helps to keep those back wheels firmly on the road. They're larger than the front's – 12.5J compared with 10.5J.

Far left: When the scissor doors are opened, it is possible to squeeze into the cockpit. The rear side windows are false.

SPECIFICATION	MERCEDES-BENZ CLK-GTR
Engine location	Mid, longitudinal
Configuration	V12
Bore and stroke	89 x 92mm
Capacity	6898cc
Valve operation	Twin overhead camshafts, 4 valves per cylinder
Horsepower	612bhp @ 6800rpm
Transmission	Six speed
Drive	Rear
Chassis	Carbon-fibre monocoque
Suspension – front	Wishbones and coil springs
Suspension – rear	Wishbones and coil springs
Brakes	Ventilated disc
Top speed	199mph (320km/h)
Acceleration	0-62mph (0-100km/h) 3.8 seconds

Mercedes-Benz SL

Despite the fact that the superbly equipped two-plus-two SL roadster appeared in 1989, it is still a head-turner and provides essential transport for the fashionably rich and famous.

Sleek, refined and fast, the SL's engines range from 2.8 to 6 litres.

CAPABLE OF an apparently effortless 155mph (249km/h), the current model is the latest of a line that began in 1954 with the famous 'gullwing' coupe. The initials then stood for sport-light, although this is hardly an appropriate tag now because the latter-day top-line SL turns the scales at 3064lb (1390kg)!

Although built on a purpose-designed floorpan, the model's front strut and multi-link rear suspension was effectively carried over from the 200/300 and 190 saloons. This much-enhanced adaptive suspension electronically adjusts its settings in accordance with road conditions.

The two-door bodywork with its distinctive, purposeful sloping grille, has an automatic hood that rises at the touch of a button. But when the stylish aluminium hardtop is fitted, the car is transformed into a snug coupe with far better aerodynamics than when the car is driven as an open vehicle.

The SL was initially available with a choice of three engines, a pair of 3 litre sixes, with 12- and 24-valve cylinder heads, and a 5 litre V8 also with twin overhead camshafts. For a time the V8 was the top-line version of the SL, and it was capable of over 170mph (274km/h) but this speed was limited, in the interests of safety, to 155mph (249km/h).

But from 1992 it was displaced as the top-of-range option by a 6 litre V12 engine, a tuned version of the unit used in the company's S-class saloons. Top speed was similarly restricted to an ultra smooth, turbine-like 155mph (249km/h).

For 1994 a lower capacity 2.8 litre six was introduced and the 3 litre was enlarged to 3.2 litres. This, along with the V8, an AMG-uprated version of the latter engine, and the V12 constitutes the current engine line.

Yet a further refinement came in 1996 with the arrival of an alternative hardtop with glass roof, which reduces light penetration to just 15 per cent to cut back glare and heat build-up.

But just how do you improve on such acknowledged excellence? Well, it would seem that Mercedes-Benz can. A new SL is scheduled for the year 2001...

Although a roadster, an impressively engineered hardtop can transform the SL into a stylish coupe.

SPECIFICATION	MERCEDES-BENZ 600 SL
Engine location	Front, in-line
Configuration	V12
Bore and stroke	89 x 80mm
Capacity	5987cc
Valve operation	Twin overhead camshafts, 4 valves per cylinder
Horsepower	395bhp @ 5000rpm
Transmission	Five speed
Drive	Rear
Chassis	Unitary
Suspension – front	MacPherson strut
Suspension – rear	Multi-link
Brakes	Disc, ventilated at front
Top speed	155mph (249km/h)
Acceleration	0-60mph (0-97km/h) 6.1 seconds

Porsche Boxster

The mid-engined Boxster roadster, introduced in 1996, combines superlative roadholding with distinctive appearance and the allure of a world-famous sporting name.

An uncompromising two-seater, because of its mid-located engine, the Boxster is well equipped, with leather upholstery available at extra cost.

CONCEIVED AS an all-important second and cheaper product to the evergreen 911 model, the Boxster began life as a concept car that appeared at the 1993 Detroit Motor Show. Its name and styling are deeply rooted in Porsche's illustrious past. The car's lines are inspired by the sports-racing 550 Spyder of the 1950s while the unusual name, rather than the customary number that Porsche normally gives its models, is a combination of boxer, the European description for a horizontally opposed engine of the type used by Porsche, and its 1950s 356-based Speedster.

The enthusiastic reception accorded to the Boxster in Detroit convinced Porsche that the model was viable. The production version closely resembles it, although some features have had to be sacrificed to the practicalities of volume manufacturing.

Consequently the production Porsche lacks the curved doors featured on the concept Boxster, its front wings are wider than the original to accommodate a radiator on each side, and the engine cooling ducts are relocated higher up the rear quarter panels, rather than at their bases.

Like its larger and more costly 911 stablemate, the Boxster is powered by a six-cylinder boxermotor, although it is mid-located rather than rear-positioned.

Of 2.5 litres capacity, the presence of those concealed radiators betrays that it is water- rather than air-cooled, a feature that was also extended to the 911 in 1997. It similarly incorporates twin overhead camshafts per bank and four valves per cylinder.

A five-speed gearbox is employed although there is an option of a Porsche-developed, competition-honed Tiptronic S automatic gearbox. Here the driver has the choice of an 'auto' mode or manual change simply by activating one of two rocker switches located in the steering wheel arms.

This Porsche is strictly a two-seater because of the engine location that provides excellent roadholding but at the expense of intrusion into the passenger space. With a top speed of 150mph (241km/h), impeccable road manners and timeless styling, the Boxster looks like being around for many years to come.

The front of the Boxster has much in common with the new 911 with which it shares many components.

SPECIFICATION	PORSCHE BOXSTER
Engine location	Mid, in-line
Configuration	6-cylinder horizontally opposed
Bore and stroke	86 x 72mm
Capacity	2480cc
Valve operation	Twin overhead camshafts, 4 valves per cylinder
Horsepower	204bhp @ 6000rpm
Transmission	Five speed
Drive	Rear
Chassis	Unitary
Suspension – front	MacPherson strut
Suspension – rear	MacPherson strut
Brakes	Ventilated disc
Top speed	150mph (241km/h)
Acceleration	0-60mph (0-97km/h) 6.8 seconds

Porsche 911 Carrera

The Porsche 911 is not only one of the world's greatest performance cars, it has also been in production for longer than other model. Announced in 1963, it has passed through many stages of evolution although its original specification has essentially survived intact.

Porsche's own Tiptronic automatic gearbox is available at extra cost. Changes are effected, competition-style, by buttons on the topmost steering wheel spokes.

THE CURRENT car is the fifth generation of the breed and all versions now carry the Carrera name introduced to the 911 in 1972. This was reserved for its more potent variants.

Work began on what was internally designated the 996 series in 1992. From the outset the new edition of the 911 was the mainstream project, while the Boxster (see page 23) was secondary to it, although it was announced first. No less than 36 per cent of components are shared between the two cars.

This latest version of the 911 is longer and wider and thus roomier than its predecessors. Every panel has been revised but, happily, there is still no doubting its ancestry. Having said that, the front and headlamps styling is clearly influenced by the Boxster, the door

windows now lack the quarter lights that had featured since 1963, and the distinctive extended rear wheel arches have disappeared.

But the most radical change is not outwardly apparent because, for the first time in the model's, and indeed the company's 51-year history, none of its cars are powered by air-cooled engines.

The resultingly quieter water-cooled, horizontally opposed, alloy six-cylinder unit shares its configuration and twin-overhead-camshaft/four-valve-per-cylinder layout with the Boxster engine. Its capacity of 3387cc is 213cc less than its predecessor's although the unit develops more power, 300 rather than 286bhp.

The new cooling arrangement means that the twin radiators are located, Boxster-like, in each front wing. Despite the presence of three intake manifolds for each cylinder head, and the complication of variable intake valve timing, the power unit is both shorter and lower than the old one.

The gearbox is a six-speed unit, while the Tiptronic S automatic has five speeds plus an additional radiator to cool the transmission fluid.

Introduced at the 1997 Frankfurt Motor Show, the new 911 initially appeared in its traditional coupe form and was given a positive thumbs up by commentators. They applauded the fact that it has been able to bridge the twin requirements of performing as a civilized grand tourer and as an out-and-out sports car. The top speed, a deceptive 174mph (280km/h), is three mph (5km/h) faster than the model it replaces while 0.2 seconds have been shaved off the 0-60mph (97km/h) figure of 5.1 seconds.

Seven months after the coupe's appearance, a cabriolet (open) version, a feature of the 911 line since 1982, was announced at the 1998 Geneva event.

Four-wheel drive, another 911 option since 1989, arrived at the 1998 Paris show, with a fearsome 500bhp turbocharged version following a year later. A Targa top model should also be in the offing. Thus reinvigorated, and after a period of uncertainty, the still independent Porsche is looking in better shape than it has done for some years as it accelerates confidently into the 21st century.

SPECIFICATION	PORSCHE 911
Engine location	Rear, in-line
Configuration	6-cylinder, horizontally opposed
Bore and stroke	96 x 78mm
Capacity	3387cc
Valve operation	Twin overhead camshafts, 4 valves per cylinder
Horsepower	296bhp @ 6800rpm
Transmission	Six speed
Drive	Rear
Chassis	Unitary
Suspension – front	MacPherson strut
Suspension – rear	Multi-link
Brakes	Disc, ventilated front
Top speed	174mph (280km/h)
Acceleration	0-60mph (0-97km/h) 4.7 seconds

Left: The seemingly immortal Porsche 911, rear-engined and therefore with some luggage space beneath the bonnet. The hood that is raised at the touch of a button stores neatly beneath a movable rear panel. This cabriolet version costs some £6500 more than the coupe.

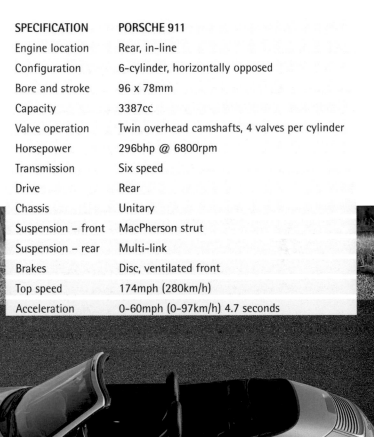

Right: As the 911's horizontally opposed engine is positioned right at the car's rear, there has always been room for the two rear seats although their backs tend to be rather upright. Air conditioning is fitted as standard, and electrically adjustable front seats are available at extra cost.

Porsche GT1

Billed as the most powerful roadgoing Porsche ever, the 544bhp GT1 coupe bears a family resemblance to the legendary 911. Created in 1997 as the roadfriendly version of the sports racer of the same name, just 30 examples were produced.

This Porsche was only produced in left-hand-drive form and has a sparsely furnished cockpit. But the Momo steering wheel is suede-trimmed!

THE GT1 competition car was created to win the Le Mans 24 hour race in which, in 1995, the McLaren F1 had triumphed. The rules stipulated that power should be limited to 600bhp and that the cars should outwardly resemble a production model. For Porsche this could only mean the 911.

Also eligible for the GT Championship, racing regulations required that a batch of road cars should be produced. Built at Porsche's Weissach motor sport division, these duly appeared in April 1997, some 10 months after the GT1's Le Mans debut.

The coupes created for the 24 hour classic event were an impressive cocktail of Porsche themes, in that they used the front floorpan of the 911 to which was grafted the rear end of the company's formidable 962 sports racer.

This combination, built up around the 911's steel substructure, was chosen because the 962 employed a mid- rather than a rear-mounted engine and the GT1 benefited from the better roadholding that resulted. It also permitted the construction of more aerodynamically efficient bodywork.

The engine configuration was 911-related although its 3.2 litre capacity, twin turbochargers and water cooling were all peculiar to the racer. Two GT1s were entered and, although not winners, they came in second and third. However, there was some compensation with the race being won by a TWR–Porsche.

The roadgoing version, of 1997, closely resembled the racers in specification although the engine had been tamed to produce 'only' 544bhp. Initially Porsche was reluctant to unleash such a projectile for road use and intended to dispense with the sport racers' twin KKK turbos so that the flat six should only develop a still very effective 300bhp. But the customers stayed away, so the Stuttgart company had little choice but to reinstate the exhaust gas-driven blowers and the performance that went with them.

Porsche claims a top speed in excess of 190mph (306km/h) for the GT1 road car. Concessions for road use include a passenger seat and the option of air conditioning. But the interior has much in common with the utilitarian Model T Ford; well-heeled customers could have any colour they wanted as long as it was black.

Priced at around £600,000, the GT1 was only available in left-hand-drive form. There's little that can match it's performance although the Mercedes-Benz CLK-GTR (see pages 20–21), built for the same GT championship, must be a strong contender.

The Porsche GT1s were back at Le Mans in 1997 but the event was essentially a re-run of the previous year. However, in 1998 Stuttgart's perseverance paid off. Although the engine and transmission were essentially carried over from the previous year, regulations required that the flat sixes should be mildly de-tuned to deliver 550bhp. The chassis of the re-designated GT1 98 was now constructed of weight-saving carbon fibre concealed beneath new aerodynamically honed bodywork.

They dominated the race and came in first and second, giving Porsche its first works victory since 1987 and its 16th Le Mans triumph. And those lucky GT1 road car owners can reflect that this was achieved with cars whose engines developed about as much power as their own...

SPECIFICATION	PORSCHE GT1
Engine location	Mid, in-line
Configuration	6-cylinder horizontally opposed, twin turbocharged
Bore and stroke	74 x 95mm
Capacity	3200cc
Valve operation	Twin overhead camshafts, 4 valves per cylinder
Horsepower	544bhp @ 7000rpm
Transmission	Six speed
Drive	Rear
Chassis	Unitary
Suspension – front	Wishbones and coil springs
Suspension – rear	Wishbones and coil springs
Brakes	Ventilated disc
Top speed	190mph (306km/h)
Acceleration	0-62mph (0-100km/h) 3.7 seconds

Above: The 911 look is apparent from the front of the GT1. This is the original 1996 version that ran at that year's and the 1997 Le Mans, although victory had to wait until 1998.

Left: A road version of the GT1, its carbon-fibre body panels all too apparent. Guaranteed to dominate any traffic light drag race, unless there is a McLaren F1 alongside, the rear is pure Porsche 962.

ITALY: GRACE AND PACE

No make is more suggestive of the speed, style and panache of the performance car than the blood red Ferrari GT, a make that dominated motor racing in the 1950 and 1960s and is still a significant force in Formula 1.

LIKE PORSCHE, this legendary marque is a post-war creation – Ferrari produced its first road car in 1947. Enzo Ferrari's first love was always racing but he was sufficiently realistic to recognize that a competition programme required finance and plenty of it! So he offered Ferrari grand tourers, that were initially closely related to his racers, for sale to an appreciative public.

The two lines soon diverged because of the technological demands of Formula 1, but the latest generation of Ferrari road cars are spiritual successors of those elegant V12-powered GTs of the late 1940s.

But Ferrari, like Rolls-Royce in its pre-war days, only produces its cars in mechanical form and these are then bodied by a specialist coachbuilder. In Ferrari's case, since 1951 this has always been Pininfarina, a company which continues to produce bodies of stunning elegance that perfectly complement the Maranello company's potent specifications.

The influence of the *carrozzeria*, as the Italian coachbuilders are known, has reached far beyond their native country, and the world's car makers have not only eagerly retained the services of Pininfarina, but also the likes of Bertone, Ital Design, Ghia and Zagato.

Since 1969 Ferrari has been owned by Fiat, which is currently custodian of almost the entire Italian motor industry. Despite a commitment to the mass market, its performance car credentials are impeccable and long-standing.

It is often forgotten that Fiat fielded a team of highly influential grand prix racers in the 1921–24 era and it was also in the forefront of research into performance-related aerodynamics in the 1930s.

Despite its preoccupation with volume production, the Colossus of Turin, as it is dubbed, can still produce sports models that reveal it has lost none of its innovation and flair.

The latest manifestation is the Fiat Coupe that is produced by Pininfarina, although the styling is Fiat's own. The Turin *carrozzeria* was also, in part, responsible for the lines of the equally well-

received Alfa Romeo Spider and GTV. Alfa is a company that has been producing sports cars almost since its birth in Milan in 1910, and in 1987 the then-state-owned business joined the growing Fiat empire.

It is to be hoped that these new Alfa Romeos will herald a new era for company and the same applies to Maserati, since 1993 also owned by Fiat. Like Ferrari, the Modena-based company introduced a sports car line to finance its Formula 1 activities.

The latest Maserati, the 3200 GT of 1999, is full of promise and only time will tell whether this is another false dawn for a company that for many years seemingly had only a dazzling past but no future to celebrate.

A new model is also promised by Lamborghini which will be all the more significant because, since 1998, it has been owned by Volkswagen. Conceived in 1963 as a rival to Ferrari by tractor manufacturer Ferruccio Lamborghini, the make has suffered switchback fortunes since he sold out in 1972. There have been a succession of owners, including the American Chrysler Corporation in the 1987–1993 era, so Volkswagen's commitment to what, like Ferrari, has become an Italian institution is to be particularly welcomed.

If nothing else, Lamborghini is now one of very few of Italy's car companies not to be owned by Fiat!

Above: The 5000GT was the first roadgoing Maserati to be V8 powered, a configuration that endures to this day. This photograph shows a 1964 example with coachwork by Allemano.

Right: Like Ferrari, Lamborghini espouses V12 power. The marque came of age in 1966 with the appearance of the Bertone-styled Miura, the world's first mid-engined road car.

Left: This Ferrari is a 1966 275 GTB longnose. Powered by the traditional V12 engine, this one was of 3.3 litres capacity. Introduced in 1964, not only was the 275 the first Ferrari to be fitted with all-independent suspension, it also featured alloy wheels, in place of wire spokes. The Pininfarina bodywork was new and 1966 models featured a lengthened nose and smaller air intake – hence the unofficial longnose designation. Top speed was over 150mph (241km/h).

Alfa Romeo GTV and Spider 3.0 litre V6

Too long in the doldrums, Alfa Romeo's image received a welcome boost in 1994 with the arrival of the visually stunning two-seater Spider and its closed GTV counterpart.

Right: The sensationally looking Alfa Romeo GTV is a rather cramped two-plus-two, while the Spider, below, is strictly a two-seater.

ARCHITECT OF this visual renaissance is Walter de Silva, director of Alfa Romeo's Centro Stile, and Enrico Fumia of Pininfarina, who undertook the commission prior to becoming head of design at Alfa's Lancia stablemate.

Based on the platform of the in-house Fiat Tipo saloon, both cars have the same wheelbase and share noses, wings, bonnets and doors although they look very different from the back. Pininfarina favoured a traditional tail but the closed car has a higher rear deck.

Both of these wedge-shaped cars have the same fascia, door panels and front seats although the Spider is strictly a two-seater and the closed car is just a two-plus-two because of a pair of minuscule back seats. Titled GTV, this stands for *Grand Turismo Veloce* (fast GT), a famous Alfa Romeo name that made a reappearance after a seven-year absence.

So what are the mechanicals concealed beneath the drop dead gorgeous lines? The base versions of these front-wheel-drive cars, launched at the 1994 Paris Motor Show, are powered by the Fiat Superfire 2 litre four-cylinder engine with four valves and twin spark plugs per cylinder. It endows the Spider with a top speed of

SPECIFICATION	ALFA ROMEO GTV 3.0 24V
Engine location	Front, transverse
Configuration	V6
Bore and stroke	93 x 72mm
Capacity	2959cc
Valve operation	Twin overhead camshafts, 4 valves per cylinder
Horsepower	220bhp @ 6300rpm
Transmission	Five speed
Drive	Front
Chassis	Unitary
Suspension – front	MacPherson strut
Suspension – rear	Multi-link
Brakes	Disc, front ventilated
Top speed	149mph (240km/h)
Acceleration	0-60mph (0-97km/h) 6.5 seconds

130mph (209km/h) although the heavier coupe, with its better aerodynamics, is slightly faster and able to reach 133mph (214km/h).

The open car also has the 192bhp 12-valve 3 litre V6 courtesy of the old 75 Cloverleaf and early 164 saloons. By contrast, for home consumption the top-line GTV uses a turbocharged 2 litre V6 tailored to Italian tax laws that endows the car with a top speed of 144mph (232km/h).

However, those coupes exported to markets where such legislation does not apply, such as the UK, are powered by the alternative 3 litre 24-valve V6 unit that makes the GTV a 149mph (240km/h) car.

The Spider's Duetto predecessor, also by Pininfarina, lasted for 33 years. With such an impressive stylistic precedent, both models have something to live up to.

Fiat Coupe

Despite the fact that this car first appeared in 1993, it still maintains an unusual visual vitality. If styling is right first time, it stays right! This attractive coupe is no sluggard either and the top-of-range 2 litre turbocharged version is capable of speeds approaching 150mph (241km/h).

Above: The current Fiat Coupe uses a five-cylinder engine available with or without a turbo.

Below: Like the in-house Alfa Romeo, this is a front-wheel-drive car.

BETTER KNOWN for its mass-produced small saloons, Fiat ventured into the world of sports cars with its mid-engined X1/9 of 1972. But Fiat's chairman, Vittorio Ghidella, thereafter decreed that the firm should only be concerned with volume sales. This diktat was set aside on his departure in 1989. It is no coincidence that this was the year in which work began on the coupe project.

Based on the floorpan of the company's best-selling Tipo saloon, the dramatic styling was the result of a competition between the corporate Centro Stile and Pininfarina.

Finally it was the in-house design, the work of head of styling Chris Bangle, that was chosen, although the interior by Pininfarina was adopted almost intact. That company was awarded the manufacturing contract and the Coupe thus carries its name on the exterior even though this might infer a stylistic responsibility!

This front-wheel-drive GT has a high boot, low nose and memorable highlights over the front and rear wheel arches which endow it with a sense of speed, even when stationary. A two-plus-two, it was initially powered by a 2 litre engine which it shared with the Tipo. Also available in 195bhp turbocharged form, this top-of-the-range model was a 140mph (225km/h) car.

Three years on, for the 1997 season, Fiat dropped the four in favour of a 2 litre five-cylinder unit, courtesy of the Bravo diesel saloon, this being its first petrol application. Available in unblown and turbocharged form, it has the advantage of being more economical and faster than the four. A few changes were made to the exterior with the introduction of a new grille and four-spoked Pininfarina-designed alloy wheels.

A five-speed gearbox had been on offer from the outset but in mid-1998 Fiat offered as an alternative a six-speed, courtesy of the Alfa Romeo GTV V6. Retailing at £22,825, this was £3000 more than the standard version which continues in production.

SPECIFICATION	FIAT COUPE 20V TURBO
Engine location	Front, transverse
Configuration	5-cylinder turbocharged
Bore and stroke	82 x 75mm
Capacity	1998cc
Valve operation	Twin overhead camshafts, 4 valves per cylinder
Horsepower	220bhp @ 5750rpm
Transmission	Five speed
Drive	Front
Chassis	Unitary
Suspension – front	Wishbones and struts
Suspension – rear	Trailing arms
Brakes	Disc, front ventilated
Top speed	148mph (238km/h)
Acceleration	0-60mph (0-97km/h) 6.2 seconds

Ferrari 355

The smallest model in Ferrari's current range, the years have dealt lightly with the mid-engined two-seater 355, first introduced to the market back in 1994.

The 355 uses a semi-automatic transmission operated by paddles positioned behind the steering wheel.

WORK ON the 355 began in 1991 and its 3496cc V8 engine was based on its 348 predecessor's 3405cc unit, an increase in capacity being attained by upping the stroke by 2mm to 87mm. Titanium connecting rods were used.

The twin overhead camshafts per bank were retained but, instead of four valves per cylinder, five (three inlet and two exhaust) were introduced. Butterfly throttle valves were fitted to each cylinder. Such ministrations allowed the engine to rev to 8500rpm, a then unprecedented figure for a normally aspirated road car.

Longitudinally positioned in a tubular space-frame, it retained its 348 predecessor's wheelbase although it was 30 per cent stiffer.

As ever Pininfarina was responsible for the styling of the aluminium and steel coupe bodywork; there was also a targa version with a detachable roof panel, which also owed something to the 348. But, significantly, the memorable multiple cooling fins set into the door panels, that also featured on the larger 512TR, were replaced by simpler dual ducting. However, the previous model's roof, window glass and front wings were carried over to the coupe.

Aerodynamic considerations were, as ever, to the fore and this also applied to the 355's underside which was fitted with a flat undertray that ran for the full length of the car. It is intended to equalize downforce front and rear so promoting stability.

The interior was completely new with a combination of modern and retro elements and a new dashboard. The six-speed gearbox operated in the customary open gate.

With a top speed of 184mph (296km/h) and 62mph (100km/h) arriving in a mere 4.2 seconds, the 355's acceleration is still stupendous, although driver and passenger cannot ignore the noisy presence of the alloy V8 that occupies the space normally used by rear seat passengers.

Left: The 355 Spider in its element. It is mechanically identical to the closed cars, although the open bodywork is complemented by an electrically powered hood.

Above: The 355 coupe – its lines were refined in the Pininfarina wind tunnel. The two-seater accommodation is defined by the presence of the mid-located V8 engine.

SPECIFICATION	FERRARI F355
Engine location	Mid, longitudinal
Configuration	V8
Bore and stroke	85 x 87mm
Capacity	3496cc
Valve operation	Twin overhead camshafts, 5 valves per cylinder
Horsepower	380bhp @ 8250rpm
Transmission	Five speed
Drive	Rear
Chassis	Tubular steel
Suspension – front	Wishbones and coil springs
Suspension – rear	Wishbones and coil springs
Brakes	Ventilated disc
Top speed	184mph (296km/h)
Acceleration	0-62mph (0-100km/h) 4.2 seconds

In 1995 the coupe was joined by the open F335 Spider. This had the distinction of being fitted with Ferrari's first power-operated hood. The work of Pininfarina, no less than six electric motors were required to raise the device, the whole operation taking about a minute to execute.

A further mechanical refinement was the fitment, from mid-1997, of a Formula 1 racing-type steering wheel with its attendant two gearchange paddles, located just behind the rim. The system differs from the steering wheel-actuated Porsche Tiptronic unit which operates an automatic gearbox complete with torque converter. The Ferrari device, by contrast, hydraulically actuates the car's existing manual gearbox and clutch.

Ferrari pioneered the system on Gilles Villeneuve's 312T2 Formula 1 car back in 1978 although it was subsequently dropped and not revived until 1989. Used with semi-automatic gearboxes, it is now commonplace on all grand prix cars.

The coupe, GTS targa and Spider constitute the current 355 model line-up, although there's a replacement waiting in the wings that is larger, but lighter and faster, than the original. Scheduled for an appearance in 1999, it will maintain the vitality of a marque that remains ever bright in an increasingly competitive world.

Ferrari 456 M

After two decades of producing mid-engined Ferraris, in 1992 the legendary Italian company once again reverted to the front-engined theme with the 456 M grand tourer. Still in production at the time of writing, the concept was extended in 1996 with the appearance of its 550 Maranello stablemate.

THE MARQUE'S legendary founder, Enzo Ferrari, was still alive in 1988 when the 456 was being designed, and he expressed some displeasure that the gearbox was to be attached directly to the front-located V12 engine. As a result, it was relegated to the rear of the car and is thus in better balance with the power unit – a development that improves the model's roadholding.

At the time the famous Maranello-based company was producing uncompromising mid-engined two-seaters, but the 456 is a more practical two-plus-two. As ever the two-seater coupe's aluminium bodywork was designed by Pininfarina and it still retains a timeless vitality.

Produced by Scaglietti in Modena, the most memorable

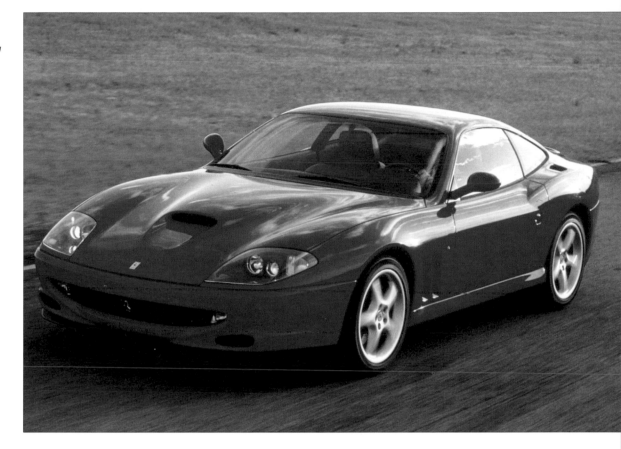

Left above: With a Ferrari even the automatic transmission operates in a handsome gate. Two-thirds of 456M customers opt for this four-speed GTA variant.

Left below: The Ferrari 456M, also front-engined but with two-plus-two accommodation, is more of a grand tourer than an out-and-out sports car.

Right: Note the 550M's lack of apparent aerodynamic aids, the windcheating lines help to give this Ferrari a top speed of 199mph (320km/h).

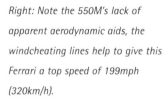

SPECIFICATION	FERRARI 456 M
Engine location	Front, in-line
Configuration	V12
Bore and stroke	88 x 75mm
Capacity	5474cc
Valve operation	Twin overhead camshafts, 4 valves per cylinder
Horsepower	436bhp @ 6250rpm
Transmission	Six speed
Drive	Rear
Chassis	Tubular steel
Suspension – front	Wishbones and coil springs
Suspension – rear	Wishbones and coil springs
Brakes	Ventilated disc
Top speed	186mph (299km/h)
Acceleration	0-60mph (0-97km/h) 5.1 seconds

features are the deep swage lines that begin at the engine hot air outlets in the front wings and which extend across the door skins and beyond. In overall terms, there are echoes of Ferrari's famous front-engined Daytona coupe of 1968–74 vintage. This cloaks a tubular all-steel chassis which at the front houses the 5.5 litre V12 engine with twin overhead camshafts per cylinder bank and four valves per cylinder. Racing-style dry sump lubrication is employed.

Ferrari's commitment to V12 power stretches back to the marque's 1947 origins. For this model the company reverted to its practice of naming its cars after the cubic capacity of one of its cylinders. In this case it is 456.19cc.

The six-speed transaxle is located at the car's rear with selection being by the traditional Ferrari open gate. Since 1996 there has been a four-speed automatic version, designated the 456M GTA.

Despite its undoubted refinement, the 456 is very much of a driver's car, with a top speed nudging 190mph (306km/h) and 60mph (97km/h) arriving in a mere 5.1 seconds.

A similar mechanical layout was applied the 456's two-seater 550 M stablemate that appeared in 1996. And while its V12 shares the same 5474cc capacity with the earlier car, it is a different story inside with lighter pistons and titanium connecting rods permitting higher revolutions. It develops 485bhp at 7000rpm which compares with the 456 which peaks at 6250rpm.

The mechanical layout is similar in configuration rather than detail to the earlier car although, as befits its more sporting proclivities, there is no automatic version.

Its Pininfarina coupe body lacks the feature lines of the 456 but is an utterly distinctive offering – thoroughly modern in design it also contains echoes of Ferrari's glorious grand tourers of the past. It thus contains retro elements aplenty.

These along with the smaller mid-engined 355 (see pages 32–33) constitute the current Ferrari range that continues to delight the motoring world at large and the fortunate few who can afford to buy and run them.

Lamborghini Diablo

Although the Diablo was announced in 1990, it still possesses all the allure of a modern supercar, with stunning lines, unfashionable thirst and uncompromising two-seater accommodation. Priced at over £186,000 in its top-line four-wheel-drive form, it is also still fabulously expensive.

CREATED AS a replacement for the Countach, introduced back in 1974, the Diablo, which is the Spanish word for devil, inherited its legendary predecessor's mechanical layout. The mighty V12 four-camshaft 48-valve engine was enlarged to 5.7 litres and, developing 492bhp, was longitudinally located in the mid-position that only allowed sufficient room for just two seats. Like the Countach, the Diablo was styled by Marcello Gandini. Top speed was anticipated at 202mph (325km/h).

The Diablo has passed through a number of phases since delivery of the first example at the beginning of 1991. In the following year of 1992 came the four-wheel-drive Diablo VT, so named because of the adoption of viscous transmission in which 17 per cent of the power was transferred to the front wheels during cornering to assist roadholding.

Lamborghini changed hands in November 1993 having been sold by Chrysler, its owner since 1987, to the Indonesian MegaTech company. That year the Diablo received some 1500 much-needed refinements, most importantly in the shape of power steering, anti-lock brakes and improvements to cabin ventilation.

In 1994 came the lightened Diablo SE 30, so named as a Special Edition model to commemorate Lamborghini's 30th anniversary as a car maker. Externally identifiable by a new front air dam and movable rear wing, the engine was reworked. Although the original capacity was retained, output was boosted to 525bhp. Top speed was a claimed 220mph (354km/h).

If the SE was a little tame for some tastes, in 1995 Lamborghini produced the Jota, which was the racing version of the Diablo, aimed at individual drivers, rather than heralding the arrival of a works team. Output of the robust V12 was again boosted, this time to 590bhp although there were few takers.

In 1996 came a long awaited open version of the Diablo. Four years in the making, it was based on the Speeder concept car exhibited at the 1992 Geneva Motor Show. Unusually the carbon-fibre roof was stored externally, above the engine.

Next, in the same year of 1996 came the SV, for Sport Veloce, version which was a lightweight Diablo, not quite as powerful as the SE, with 'only' 508bhp on tap. Outwardly identifiable by a larger rear aerofoil to generate more downforce, acceleration was

an improvement on past performance on account of lower gearing. But top speed dropped to 183mph (295km/h).

Later came the sport racing SV-based Diablo GT2 with the V12 boosted to an eye-watering 640bhp. A roadgoing version with the long-running V12 stretched to 6 litres appeared in 1998 with lighter carbon-fibre body panels.

The current Lamborghini range consists of the Diablo coupes and roadster which are available in SV and four-wheel-drive VT forms. They now share the same 5.7 litre 530bhp engines.

Then, to universal surprise, Lamborghini was sold, in July 1998, to an expansive Volkswagen and allocated to its Audi arm. The new management decided to put a projected Super Diablo on hold so the existing models look like being around for some while yet

SPECIFICATION	LAMBORGHINI DIABLO SV
Engine location	Mid, in-line
Configuration	V12
Bore and stroke	87 x 80mm
Capacity	5707cc
Valve operation	Twin overhead camshafts, 4 valves per cylinder
Horsepower	530bhp @ 7000rpm
Transmission	Five speed
Drive	Rear
Chassis	Tubular steel
Suspension – front	Wishbones and coil springs
Suspension – rear	Wishbones and coil springs
Brakes	Disc, front ventilated
Top speed	200mph (322km/h)
Acceleration	0-60mph (0-97km/h) 4.4 seconds

Maserati 3200 GT

The Maserati make has been effectively re-born with the launch at the 1998 Paris Motor Show of the 3200 GT coupe. With svelte, distinctive styling and a top speed of over 170mph (274km/h), this latest model from Modena is the first outward evidence of its Fiat parent's commitment to the marque.

Leather is extensively used in the new Maserati, evidence of in-house Ferrari's influence. The Momo steering wheel is shared with the latter's 456.

MASERATI, ESTABLISHED in 1926, was best known for superlative racing cars until its withdrawal from Formula 1 competition at the end of 1957. A modest low-volume road car line was established after the Second World War to help finance this competition programme and the first significant model was the 3500 GT of 1958, the inspiration for the new coupe.

In 1993 the company, which had been run since 1975 and later owned by the controversial de Tomaso, was acquired by Fiat. Four years later, in 1997, Maserati was brought under the control of its one-time rival but now in-house stablemate, Ferrari. The two makes will be complementary with Maserati concentrating on grand tourers rather than sports cars; a saloon will be ongoing and the range priced at around 25 per cent less than Ferrari's.

Apart from its V8 engine, that has been extensively revised, the 3200 GT is a completely new car with its own floorpan, suspension and body. In addition Fiat has invested the equivalent of £7 million on rebuilding Maserati's Modena factory. Build quality,

The styling by Giorgetto Giugiario's Ital Design manages to combine a sense of tradition with a shape to take the revitalized marque into the 21st century. The substructure is also new; only the 3.2 V8 engine has been carried over and that has been extensively re-worked.

A sight that drivers will have to get used to as a 3200 sweeps past them! The hockey stick rear lights are the only radical aspect of what is otherwise a very conservative design. They are the hallmark of Fiat, Maserati's corporate parent.

once a bugbear of the marque, is now regarded as being on a par with the best of its European and Japanese rivals.

Work on the project began soon after the Fiat take-over of 1993. The all-important body is stylistically the work of Giorgetto Giugiario's Ital Design. He was chosen in preference to Marcello Gandini who had essayed, among other Maseratis, the Quattroporte saloon which remains in production.

A well-proportioned coupe, but not a hatchback, with distinctive 'hockey stick' rear lights, the contours reveal the influence of extensive wind-tunnel testing.

Inside the two-plus-two, the rear seats really are functional, the interior is well-appointed but visually restrained in execution, and the Ferrari influence is apparent. When it took over the Maserati brief, it initiated a complete redesign and replaced with leather the existing wood on the steering wheel, handbrake, gearlever and dashboard. The ergonomics were also revised.

The company claims that 90 per cent of the 3.2 litre V8, which uses twin overhead camshafts per cylinder bank, is new. Twin turbocharged, like the previous generation of Maserati models, great care has been taken to refine their application so that the abrupt cut-in of the earlier radial-flow blowers has been replaced by more responsive variable-flow IHI units. The company claims a

0-62mph (100km/h) figure of just 5.1 seconds and a 174mph (280km/h) top speed.

Production began at the beginning of 1999. Providing this car has been completely de-bugged and build quality is up to the promised quality, it will truly herald a new dawn for the marque. It is targeted at a market sector at present comfortably occupied by the Jaguar XK8, Aston Martin DB7 and Porsche 911.

Capitalizing on this coupe and an impending cabriolet, Maserati hopes that it will sell 6000 cars a year by 2002. Fiat, for one, hopes this will be the case.

SPECIFICATION	MASERATI 3200 GT
Engine location	Front, in-line
Configuration	V8 twin turbocharged
Bore and stroke	80 x 80mm
Capacity	3217cc
Valve operation	Twin overhead camshafts, 4 valves per cylinder
Horsepower	370bhp @ 6250rpm
Transmission	Six speed
Drive	Rear
Chassis	Unitary
Suspension – front	Wishbones and coil springs
Suspension – rear	Wishbones and coil springs
Brakes	Ventilated disc
Top speed	174mph (280km/h)
Acceleration	0-62mph (0-100km/h) 5.1 seconds

JAPAN: SPEED BY DESIGN

 Still the world's largest motor-manufacturing nation, Japan's automotive industry is essentially a post-war phenomenon, even though Toyota, Mitsubishi and Nissan can trace their respective origins further back to 1936, 1917 and 1912.

HOWEVER, IT was Honda, which did not join the ranks of Japan's car makers until 1962, that has the longest-standing commitment to the performance sector.

By then the world's largest manufacturer of motorcycles and with an enviable racing record on two wheels, in 1966 Honda launched its S600 sports two-seater. Only destined to survive for four years, in 1999 Honda returns to the lower-cost quantity sports car market with the conventional rear-drive S2000 roadster. This new model will appear in conjunction with Honda's long-anticipated re-entry to Formula 1 racing at the beginning of the 2000 season.

Now Toyota, not only Japan's, but the world's, largest car maker, is tipped to follow Honda and make its grand prix debut in 2002. Its sortie into the world of performance motoring came in 1965 with the low-volume 2000 GT coupe but its first significant sports car debuted in 1984 with the mid-engined MR2, a respected model that survives to this day.

Toyota has also sought to win the Le Mans 24 hour race and in 1997 one of its TS20 sports racers was placed ninth, six positions behind its Nissan rival.

That company was the manufacturer of the famous 240Z coupe of 1969, although it was then badged as a Datsun. It went on to become the world's best-selling sports car and spawned 260

Above: Honda's S800 sports car, only 791cc but capable of 95mph (153km/h). This is a 1970 example.

and 280 derivatives. Nissan is reported to be contemplating a revival of its Z car line.

It has supported rallying with works teams since the 1970s, but although putting up some strong performances, the world championship laurels have eluded it. The prize was grasped by Toyota which, in 1993, became the first Japanese manufacturer to win the title with its Celica Turbo. But in the following three years this accolade went to Subaru.

Part of Fiju Heavy Industries, Subaru is a long-standing advocate of the flat (horizontally opposed) engine, a characteristic that it shares with Porsche, although its power units are front- rather than rear- or mid-located.

In 1998 the world rally championship again went to a Japanese car maker in the form of Mitsubishi, a company that can trace its motor car origins back to 1917, although the present generation dates from 1959. Its first true performance car was the Starion 2000 of 1982 but the Lancer that triumphed in the '98 rally season was a world away from that potent though turbo-lagged coupe.

All these companies are Japanese-owned, but in 1996 Mazda was bought by Ford. The Toyo Kogyo company began building trucks in 1931 and added cars to its growing corporate portfolio in 1960. In 1967 it launched a pioneering twin-Wankel-powered sports coupe and persevered with rotary power long after it had been abandoned by other car makers.

But far more influential was Mazda's Japanese/American-designed low-cost MX-5 sports car of 1989 that was as conventional as its RX Wankel-engined series cars had been unorthodox.

Interestingly Suzuki, another Japanese motorcycle manufacturer, joined the ranks of car makers in 1961 with a diminutive but ingenious range, of which the wacky Cappuccino is an example, which is another variant of the widely imitated MX-5 concept.

As in so many other instances in the motor industry, others now follow where Japan has led, both at home and abroad.

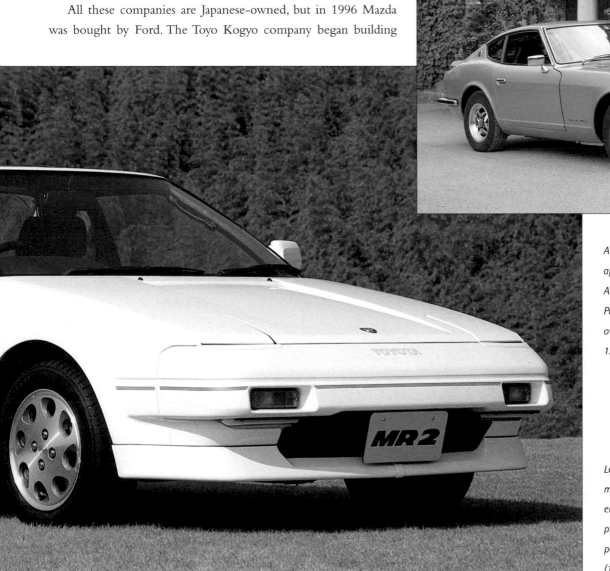

Above: Nissan's Datsun 240Z appeared in 1969 and took the American sports car market by storm. Powered by a 2.4 litre, six-cylinder, overhead-cam engine, it could attain 125mph (201km/h).

Left: The Toyota MR2 of 1984 with its mid-located, 1.6 litre, twin-cam engine combined impressive, predictable handling with good performance. Top speed was 120mph (193km/h).

Honda S2000

While Honda is best known for its prestigious mid-engined NSX performance car, it is returning to the popular sports car market with the launch, in 1999, of the S2000 roadster.

It went that-a-way! The Honda's soon to be familiar neat and distinctive rear.

THE MODEL'S origins are to be found in the SSM, an abbreviation which stands for Sports Study Model, that appeared at 1995 Tokyo Motor Show. Acclaimed as the star of the event, this open two-seater concept car was powered by a 2 litre five-cylinder engine that drove the rear wheels.

But beneath the sleek body was a space-frame chassis and suspension courtesy of the NSX coupe. A novel but impractical feature was a two-cockpit design which, although visually attractive, restricted shoulder room for both driver and passenger.

Three years later, at the 1998 Paris show, the European public had the opportunity of viewing the S2000 prototype in advance of the model actually entering production in January 1999 at the same purpose-built plant in which the NSX is assembled.

In overall, if not detail, terms, the car is clearly inspired by the '95 Tokyo show exhibit, although most of its more novel features have succumbed to the practicalities of the production line.

The essentials of the north/south engine layout driving the rear wheels have survived, but the 2 litre five has been replaced by a four-cylinder unit with the customary twin overhead camshafts and their attendant 16 valves. Employing variable valve timing, the unit develops over 240bhp which is a particularly impressive figure for a engine of that capacity. It is located behind the front axle line

with the result that the car has a 50/50 weight distribution between the power unit and rear drive assembly.

But because of the driven rear wheels, and as Honda only otherwise produces a range of transversely engined front-wheel-drive saloons, the S2000 has a purpose-designed platform and transmission train. The last Honda to employ this engine/drive configuration was the S800 sports car of 1966–71 vintage and Honda has revived the practice of adopting the S, for sport, prefix followed by the cubic capacity of its engine for the new model.

But the space-frame of the SSM concept has been discarded, along with the distinctive but impractical two-cockpit cabin, although the body lines survive in spirit rather than in detail.

The low-mounted and distinctive headlamps have been transferred to a more conventional location in the front wings in deference to Japan's traffic laws. But in general, the S2000 has been designed for world markets, most significantly the lucrative North American one, and it will also go on sale in Europe.

The engine is started by the driver pressing a large button to the right of the steering column; there are digital display instruments and a power-operated hood. The large central transmission tunnel is a distinctive feature.

The S2000's announcement was timed to coincide with the 50th anniversary of Honda's birth in 1949 which fell on 24th September 1999, a week before the Paris launch.

With such a vehicle the company intends to rekindle the pleasures of driving and it also underlines its commitment to motorsport. Honda is also intending to return to Formula 1 racing for the first time since 1968, while its engines powered the World Championship-winning Williams in 1986/7 and McLaren in four successive seasons between 1988 and 1991.

Below: The 2000's side elevation clearly underlines that the four-cylinder engine is located behind the front axle line. The wedge profile is also apparent.

Right: The S2000 is an uncompromising two-seater. Honda has forsaken its traditional front-wheel-drive for a more traditional front-engine/rear-drive layout.

SPECIFICATION	HONDA S2000
Engine location	Front, in-line
Configuration	4-cylinder
Bore and stroke	87 x 84mm
Capacity	1997cc
Valve operation	Twin overhead camshafts, 4 valves per cylinder
Horsepower	237bhp @ 8500rpm
Transmission	Six speed
Drive	Rear
Chassis	Unitary
Suspension – front	Wishbones and coil springs
Suspension – rear	Wishbones and coil springs
Brakes	Ventilated disc
Top speed	150mph (241km/h)
Acceleration	0-60mph (0-97km/h) 5.5 seconds

Mazda MX-5

In 1989 Mazda, in the face of considerable scepticism from its fellow car makers, introduced its no-frills open two-seater: the MX-5 sports car. It proved to be a great success on both sides of the Atlantic and spawned a host of imitators. By the time it was subtly updated for the 1998 season, no less than 430,000 examples had been built.

Above: The in-line twin-cam four is available in 1.6 and 1.8 litre forms and the latest MX-5 has been enhanced by the fitment of new inlet and exhaust systems.

CREATED AT Mazda North America's product planning and research facility at Irvine, California, the original MX-5 was conceived as a latter-day version of classic British sports cars of the 1960s, most significantly the Triumph Spitfire and Lotus Elan.

The resulting Japanese-built car, aimed foursquare at the lucrative American sports car market, was widely acclaimed throughout the world for its no-nonsense mechanicals and front engine/rear drive configuration.

At the MX-5's heart was Mazda's proven 1.6 litre, twin-overhead-camshaft, four-cylinder, longitudinally located engine that had hitherto been mounted transversely in the company's front-wheel-drive saloon range. Top speed was 115mph (185km/h).

But in the new sports car the drive was conveyed, via a torque tube, to the rear wheels. Suspension, by wishbones and coil springs, was independent all round, a feature that the MX-5 shared with its British progenitors.

These mechanical components were integrated in a neat though distinctive open two-seater body with fashionable pop-up headlamps. The original MX-5 Miata, as it was billed in the 'States, was offered with an alternative 1.8 litre engine for the 1994 season. By the time that production ceased in 1997, Mazda was effectively dominating the class it had created.

The new version of the MX-5 was introduced for the 1998 model year and, while the proven formula was perpetuated, the new version differed – modestly rather than radically – from the original. Unlike the first MX-5, this car was redesigned and engineered in Japan.

The most obvious difference is the deletion of the pop-up headlamps and their replacement by conventional units, undertaken, said the company, to save weight. Having said that, every panel in the slightly wider open two-seater body has been reworked. It is also much stronger than its predecessor, and there is now better side-impact protection, which has added weight.

The original sub-structure has been retained. However, the car's behaviour differs from the original in that, while the suspension has been carried over, the settings have been changed to increase stability yet without losing the universally praised sense

SPECIFICATION	MAZDA MX-5 1.8i S
Engine location	Front, in-line
Configuration	4-cylinder
Bore and stroke	83 x 85mm
Capacity	1839cc
Valve operation	Twin overhead camshafts, 4 valves per cylinder
Horsepower	140bhp @ 6500rpm
Transmission	Five speed
Drive	Rear
Chassis	Unitary
Suspension – front	Wishbones and coil springs
Suspension – rear	Wishbones and coil springs
Brakes	Ventilated disc
Top speed	128mph (206km/h)
Acceleration	0-62mph (0-100km/h) 8 seconds

of excitement that driving the car generates. As before, the MX-5 is built in 1.6 and 1.8 litre forms, and while, mechanically, these twin-overhead-camshaft, 16-valve units are essentially carried over, they do develop more power. Power output in the smaller capacity four is up from 116 to 125bhp. The 1.8 is fitted with a variable intake system and it produces 140bhp.

But unlike the first generation MX-5, which was fitted with a five-speed manual gearbox, the Mark II version has a new six-speeder with a gear change that is just as good as original.

On the road Mazda has managed to perpetuate the sense of fun that made the original car so popular. Steering response is, as ever, impeccable. For the price – its sells for £15,500 in Britain – the MX-5 has few peers.

Left: An MX-5 with its manually operated hood raised. It is improved by the fitment of a heated glass rear window in place of the original's flexible one.

Right: This latest version is identifiable by its headlamps – its predecessor featured pop-up units. Otherwise the lines are similar but subtly enhanced. Body-coloured door handles replace chromed units. Less outwardly apparent are the chassis improvements.

Mitsubishi 3000GT

Although Mitsubishi's 3000GT was launched as long ago as 1990, this flagship coupe is still competitive and bristles with such technicalities as four-wheel-drive, four-wheel steering and computer-controlled suspension and braking.

Right: The driver's seat is power-operated allowing adjustments for leg room, height and even side support.

Right below: With four-wheel drive and steering, a computer keeps each shock absorber correctly trimmed, based on speed, steering and brakes.

Below: Each bank of three cylinders has its own turbocharger and intercooler.

THE MODEL'S origins are to be found in the experimental HSX sports coupe that Mitsubishi unveiled at the 1989 Tokyo Motor Show. It featured the electronic and mechanical refinements listed above, but the coupe body was deceptive and suggested a mid-engine location.

In fact the air intakes positioned ahead of the rear wheels were intended to cool the brakes, and the power unit was, in fact, transversely mounted at the front of the vehicle.

Developed jointly with its Chrysler partner, a liaison forged in 1971, what was initially known as the Mitsubishi Starion GTO emerged in 1990 as a production car based on the Japanese company's acclaimed Sigma saloon, voted Japanese Car of the Year in 1991, from which it inherited its advanced specifications. This Mitsubishi dubbed as its 'integrated driving system'.

The 3 litre V6 engine with twin overhead camshafts, and the attendant four valves per cylinder, was similarly sourced. But in the coupe it was twin-turbocharged, with the result that power rose from 202bhp to 300bhp. This resulted a 0-60mph (97km/h) figure of 5.6 seconds and top speed a blistering 155mph (249km/h).

While the model's mechanicals were Japanese, the sleek body lines were the work of Chrysler's Tom Gale and they were conceived in its Pacific studio. Sold in the 'States as the Dodge Stealth, it outwardly differed from the Japanese version but both were enhanced by the presence of a ground-effect front spoiler that extended downwards by 50 degrees at speeds above 50mph (80km/h). Simultaneously the rear wing spoiler changed its profile by 14 degrees to increase downforce. Unusually, the exhaust note could be tuned from a button on the dashboard!

The high tech theme was extended to the two-plus-two interior. There was even a TV screen to inform the driver to which part of the cabin the air-conditioned ventilation reached. However, the sophisticated audio system was viewed as being bafflingly complex by some bewildered owners.

Known outside Japan as the 3000 GT, over the years some changes have been made to the specification, although the four-wheel-drive and steering system has remained essentially the same.

For the 1994 season Mitsubishi responded to the appearance of a rival, the considerably cheaper Toyota Supra, by boosting the GT's engine output to 320bhp. This, and the fitment of a new close-ratio six-speed Getrag gearbox, helped to improve acceleration although the 155mph (249km/h) top speed remained the same.

Simultaneously, the original pop-up headlamps were replaced by flush-fitting units, and there was a revised air intake and the feature lines on the lower body sides were remodelled.

By 1995 engine power had been slightly reduced, to 281bhp, and the following year saw the arrival of a Spyder convertible version, although this is confined to the American market.

This big coupe is an assured performer with tremendous grip in the dry, a characteristic that is even more apparent in the wet. But on the debit side some commentators have found the engine a little sluggish at low speeds, as the transmission takes up. And the electronic gizmos have contributed to make this Mitsubishi a heavy car; it turns the scales at a substantial 3792lb (1720kg)...

SPECIFICATION	MITSUBISHI 3000GT
Engine location	Front, transverse
Configuration	V6, twin turbocharged
Bore and stroke	91 x 76mm
Capacity	2972cc
Valve operation	Twin overhead camshafts, 4 valves per cylinder
Horsepower	281bhp @ 6000rpm
Transmission	Six speed
Drive	Four wheel
Chassis	Unitary
Suspension – front	MacPherson strut
Suspension – rear	Wishbones, trailing arms
Brakes	Ventilated disc
Top speed	155mph (249km/h)
Acceleration	0-60mph (0-97km/h) 5.6 seconds

Nissan R390 GT1

Victory in the Le Mans 24 hour race has proved an alluring goal for motor manufacturers. And happily for the public this quest has spawned a new generation of fabulous road cars of which the Mercedes-Benz CLK-GTR and Porsche GT1 are two outstanding European examples.

Right: It doesn't look like the Nissans you see every day on the roads, but they're not designed to win Le Mans. The light, strong bodywork is a carbon-fibre/Kevlar combination.

Below: That purposeful tail with its pronounced lip to generate downforce conceals a 3.5 litre turbocharged V8 engine. There are minuscule cubby-holes located above each tail light.

THE LURE of a victory in the 24 hour classic event also encouraged Nissan to throw its hat in the ring and the result is the R390 GT1. About the only resemblance it has to the cars you'll encounter in the dealer showrooms are a handful of components and the marque name.

It is one of the most expensive and exotic vehicles yet produced by a Japanese car maker. A trio of the mid-engined V8 coupes was run at Le Mans in 1997 and, despite one putting up the fastest qualifying time, they all suffered from overheated gearboxes. One car did complete the race but came in a lowly 12th.

The roadgoing version that was announced in May 1998, just prior to the race, is effectively a detuned version of the sports racer. Many lessons were learnt following the previous year's sortie to the Sarthe circuit.

The cars are not designed in Japan but Britain, being engineered by the Oxfordshire-based TWR Group, which was responsible for the Le Mans-winning XJR Jaguars, in conjunction with Nissan Motorsport International. Styling is the work of Ian Callum who has the acclaimed lines of the Aston Martin DB7 to his credit.

Beneath the sleek carbon-fibre/Kevlar monocoque is a purpose-designed, longitudinally located, twin-turbocharged, 3.5 litre V8 engine mounted amidships. It develops 350bhp but the racing R390 produces a fearsome 600bhp. A six-speed sequential gearbox is employed.

The suspension, which uses double wishbones and coil springs, has also been softened for road use. Changes have been made to the front of the '98 cars to improve airflow around the radiators. Air is then extracted from vents just ahead of the windscreen pillars.

But the principal differences between the two cars is that the later version had a tail 4.7 inches (120mm) longer than the original.

In the roadgoing form this Nissan is 'only' capable of 155mph (249km/h). The interior is leather-trimmed and the only cabin features that bear any relationship to Nissan's current passenger line are the steering wheel and switches. Outside the car's headlamps are courtesy of the 300ZX.

Le Mans is held in June and in 1998 once again Nissan entered a trio of R390s. It was an impressive entry because all finished, with the top-placed Nissan coming in third behind two Porsche GT1s. The crew became the first all-Japanese team to mount the Le Mans winner's podium. The two other cars came in fifth and sixth.

With such a good showing on only the second time out, Nissan has its sights trained on victory. But then so did rivals Toyota…

The intention was to improve aerodynamics and thus downforce. This has allowed the TWR team to transfer the small luggage bins from the centre of the car, where they may have contributed to the gearbox overheating problems, to the vehicle's rear.

SPECIFICATION	NISSAN R390 GT1
Engine location	Mid, longitudinal
Configuration	V8, twin turbocharged
Bore and stroke	85 x 77mm
Capacity	3500cc
Valve operation	Twin overhead camshafts, 4 valves per cylinder
Horsepower	350bhp @ 6500rpm
Transmission	Six speed
Drive	Rear
Chassis	Carbon fibre/Kevlar monocoque
Suspension – front	Wishbones and coil springs
Suspension – rear	Wishbones and coil springs
Brakes	Ventilated disc
Top speed	155mph (249km/h)
Acceleration	0-60mph (0-97km/h) 4.3 seconds

Subaru Impreza 22B-STi

Subaru won the coveted world rally championship in the three years between 1995 and 1997. Although it did not repeat this success in 1998, its top driver, Colin McRae, nevertheless won the Portugal, Corsica, and Acropolis events and was well placed in the Monte Carlo and San Remo rallies.

Above: The matt-black instrument panel closely resembles that of Subaru's world rally car. The speedometers of the replicas sold on the British market have their dials recalibrated in mph rather than kph.

TO CELEBRATE these triumphs just 424 replicas of his Impreza 22B-STi have been built for sale mostly on the Japanese market. Britain has been allocated a mere 16 examples.

Priced at £39,950, this is some £8000 less than the 22B-STi cars that reach the country unofficially, so-called 'grey imports', a practice that Subaru UK clearly takes very seriously.

The quirky four-wheel-drive Impreza first appeared in 1993 in two body styles, namely as a four-door saloon and five-door estate car. Power came from 1.6 or 1.8 litre, horizontally opposed, four-cylinder engines, or a top-of-the-range turbocharged 2 litre.

A coupe version appeared in 1994 and this represents the starting point of the 22B. At this time Subaru was beginning to

make its mark in international rallying, and in 1995 it won the rally championship title for the first time.

This and subsequent successes boosted Impreza sales but these 22B-STs differ from the mainstream cars in being virtually

Left: The Sonic Blue body and gold-finished forged aluminium wheels mirror Subaru's Impreza world rally car. The large bumper and low-mounted lamps also reflect its rally pedigree.

Above: A bird's eye view of a 22B which reveals the size of the front spoiler and its manually activated rear counterpart. The latter operates in two stages to generate extra downforce under varying conditions.

handbuilt by Subaru Tecnica International, which is the company's motorsport division.

Sonic Blue paintwork and gold-coloured forged multi-spoke aluminium wheels echo the livery of the successful world rally car. A large front bumper is integrated with the radiator grille, which is mirrored by the equally substantial manually operated rear spoiler which can be moved through a 17 degree arc to provide positive groundforce under varying conditions.

The interior features bucket seats emblazoned with the STi emblem, and blue/black seat and door trim echoes the exterior livery. The comprehensively equipped instrument panel also recalls that of the world rally car.

Those examples being sold in the UK will be specially modified for customers' individual requirements by Prodrive of Banbury, Oxfordshire which prepares all Subaru's rally cars.

The 2.2 litre 'flat' four engine, with twin overhead camshafts per cylinder bank, is based on the company's 2 litre turbocharged domestic unit. Although Subaru claims the rally-prepared engine develops 280bhp, it is thought that this figure is quoted to meet Japanese regulations and that the power unit's true output is nearer the 350bhp mark.

The four-wheel-drive system includes a cross-ratio transmission device which gives the driver control of the central differential. This transfer ratio can accordingly be changed from free to locked.

Suspension revisions include the fitment of Bilstein inverted damper struts to complement the Eibach coil springs.

This outwardly rather ordinary, but mechanically unorthodox, car has made Subaru a globally respected make. As a three times world championship winner, it is Japan's most successful participant in international rallying, although is currently being strongly challenged by Mitsubishi which took the victory laurels in 1998.

SPECIFICATION	SUBARU IMPREZA 22B-STi
Engine location	Front, in-line
Configuration	4-cylinder, horizontally opposed
Bore and stroke	96 x 75mm
Capacity	2212cc
Valve operation	Twin overhead camshafts, 4 valves per cylinder
Horsepower	280bhp @ 6000rpm
Transmission	Five speed
Drive	Four wheel
Chassis	Unitary
Suspension – front	MacPherson strut
Suspension – rear	Trailing arm, strut
Brakes	Disc, ventilated front
Top speed	Not available
Acceleration	Not available

Suzuki Cappuccino

A three-cylinder 657cc engine doesn't sound as though it could pull the skin off the proverbial rice pudding but such a unit powers Suzuki's wacky pint-sized Cappuccino to great effect.

Despite being of only 657cc, the Cappuccino's small four provides plenty of torque and flexibility.

THE MICRO car is a peculiarly Japanese phenomenon and dates from the early post-war years when the country's motor industry was struggling to assert itself. In 1951 the government introduced the so-called K-class, which stands for *Kei-Jidosha*, meaning small car. The incentive was that the resulting miniatures would be freed from rigorous city parking regulations.

Engine capacity was limited to just 360cc, but this subsequently rose to 660cc, so the Cappuccino is 3cc inside the ceiling. Further restrictions demanded that such cars should be no more than 10ft

10in (3302mm) in length, power was restricted to 65bhp and top speed to 87mph (140km/h).

Motorcycle manufacturer Suzuki has plenty of experience in extracting the maximum output from small-capacity engines and the Cappuccino has its origins in a concept car of the same name that appeared at the 1989 Tokyo Motor Show.

It was powered by a 550cc twin-cam, three-cylinder engine and, at 1056lb (479kg), weighed about as much as one of Suzuki's larger motorcycles. This was largely because of the car's carbon-

Left: The Cappuccino with its targa-style roof in place. The occupants benefit from air conditioning.

Above: The car's neat appearance revealed when the roof is removed. But the boot is minuscule!

fibre substructure and body panels that were made from a similar weight-saving material.

But by the time that the car entered production in 1991, these desirable but costly components had been replaced by steel, while the bonnet, boot and spoiler were made of aluminium. In view of this increased weight, the capacity of the triple pot engine was increased by 107cc to 657cc.

This is a similarly turbocharged twin-overhead-camshaft unit with four valves per cylinder. Developing 63.1bhp, the figure was the equivalent of an impressive 96bhp per litre.

Turning the scales at a modest 1598lb (725kg), the rear-drive open two-seater is capable of carrying its occupants to a restricted top speed of 83mph (134km/h), and in the process providing them with a good helping of fun and exhilaration.

One of the Cappuccino's most notable features is its detachable hardtop which enables four configuration options. It can be altered in a matter of minutes from a coupe to a T-bar roadster, and so to a targa-type top, or breezy open two-seater.

Despite its diminutive dimensions, this Suzuki is well equipped with all-round anti-lock disc brakes, alloy wheels and electrically adjustable leather-trimmed seats. The comprehensive specification also included air conditioning and electrically operated windows. The Cappuccino is about the same size as MG's much loved Midget, it can rev to 8500rpm and steering and roadholding would be a credit to a larger car.

Available in Britain for an 18-month period in 1993–95, the Cappuccino is still in production for the home market. The little Suzuki, of which over 100,000 have been built, has brought a breath of fresh air to the sports car world: there is nothing frothy about this particular Japanese cup of coffee.

SPECIFICATION	SUZUKI CAPPUCCINO
Engine location	Front, in-line
Configuration	3-cylinder turbocharged
Bore and stroke	65 x 66mm
Capacity	657cc
Valve operation	Twin overhead camshafts, 4 valves per cylinder
Horsepower	63bhp @ 6500rpm
Transmission	Five speed
Drive	Rear
Chassis	Unitary
Suspension – front	Wishbone and coil springs
Suspension – rear	Wishbone and coil springs
Brakes	Ventilated disc
Top speed	83mph (134km/h)
Acceleration	0-60mph (0-97km/h) 8 seconds

Honda NSX

Although Honda's flagship mid-engined NSX dates from 1990, it still exudes the engineering excellence for which this Japanese manufacturer is justifiably world famous.

The NSX's acclaimed driving position – the V6 engine is located behind driver and passenger.

HONDA CLEARLY took the project very seriously because work on this prestigious car began in 1984 and it was 1990 before it entered production.

Manufacture was assigned to a purpose-built factory at Tochigi, a plant that will also build the cheaper S2000 roadster (see pages 42–43) that appears in 1999.

Aluminium features extensively in the NSX's construction, namely in the body panels and much of 3 litre V6 twin-overhead-camshaft engine. The handsome forged wishbones in the suspension are also made from the same material.

The power unit is mounted transversely behind the driver, so this Honda is an uncompromising two-seater. The configuration endows the 160mph (257km/h) NSX with superlative handling. However, the most disappointing aspect of the car is that its fine engineering qualities are not reflected in the rather anonymous, slab-sided styling.

SPECIFICATION	HONDA NSX
Engine location	Mid, transverse
Configuration	V6
Bore and stroke	90 x 78mm
Capacity	2977cc
Valve operation	Twin overhead camshafts, 4 valves per cylinder
Horsepower	270bhp @ 7100rpm
Transmission	Five speed
Drive	Rear
Chassis	Unitary
Suspension – front	Wishbone and coil springs
Suspension – rear	Wishbone and coil springs
Brakes	Ventilated disc
Top speed	160mph (257km/h)
Acceleration	0-60mph (0-97km/h) 5.5 seconds

In 1992 a supplementary lightweight version appeared and the V6 engine was tuned and enlarged to 3.2 litre. Top speed rose to 170mph (274km/h) and 0.9 of a second was shaved off the 0-60mph (97km/h) figure which fell from 5.9 to 5 seconds. Further revisions were made in 1995 with the options of a targa-type detachable roof and a semi-automatic gearbox to replace the fully automatic version originally specified.

Further improvement arrived in 1997 with the 3.2 litre engine, that had hitherto been confined to the lightweight version, offered as an option in the mainstream NSX. It was coupled with a six-speed gearbox.

This slow-selling model must now be nearing the end of its production life and it seems unlikely that Honda will be tempted to repeat the exercise. After all, Formula 1 beckons!

Left: Honda's supercar is produced in two forms. The version with the targa-type roof in the background is designated the NSX-T. Aluminium bodywork is a feature of both models.

Toyota Supra

The fourth-generation Supra took, like the Honda NSX, many years to develop – launched in 1992, work on the project had begun as far back as 1984.

The Supra's potent twin-turbocharged six-cylinder engine provides plenty of top-end surge.

WHEN TOYOTA'S chief engineer, Isao Tsuzuki, began to contemplate a new Supra he sought to harness the power of a Chevrolet Corvette with the refinement of Honda's impending NSX. But after testing some of the world's fastest performance cars, he opted for a conventional front engine/rear drive layout.

Tsuzuki decided to make weight-saving a key element of his design philosophy and the finished product weighed 308lb (140kg) less than its predecessor. This was attained by such expedients as using one exhaust pipe instead of two, an aluminium bonnet, plastic fuel tanks, hollowed head bolts and even fitting some much publicized carpets with hollow fibres! As a result the Supra attained the best power to weight ratio in its class.

Weight considerations resulted in a V6 unit rather than a V8. Its size also permitted the fitment of twin turbochargers, although the model was also available in unblown form.

This 3 litre engine featured an iron block with twin-cam alloy heads that developed a healthy 320bhp or 220bhp shorn of its turbos. The manual gearbox had six speeds, a familiar feature these days but less common back in 1992.

The coupe hatchback body with its distinctive rear spoiler, that was an optional fitment on the turbo Supra, was a great improvement on its rather dated predecessor. But the same could not be said of the stark two-plus-two interior.

The top speed of 155mph (249km/h) was electronically limited; the true unrestricted figure was nearer 185mph (298km/h). Performance was therefore impressive and the steering excellent.

This specification proved to be remarkably enduring and the Supra continued in production as a rather more practical and glamorous stablemate to Toyota's mid-engined MR2 two-seater until production ceased in 1997.

Above: Impressive mechanicals are complemented by the Supra's bodywork, while the well-engineered chassis endows this Toyota with excellent roadholding. Alloy wheels are a desirable option.

SPECIFICATION	TOYOTA SUPRA
Engine location	Front, in-line
Configuration	6-cylinder turbocharged
Bore and stroke	86 x 86mm
Capacity	2997cc
Valve operation	Twin overhead camshafts, 4 valves per cylinder
Horsepower	326bhp @ 4800rpm
Transmission	Six speed
Drive	Rear
Chassis	Unitary
Suspension – front	Wishbone and coil springs
Suspension – rear	Wishbone and coil springs
Brakes	Ventilated disc
Top speed	155mph (249km/h)
Acceleration	0-60mph (0-97km/h) 5.3 seconds

Toyota MR-S

Destined to replace the familiar MR2 coupe in 1999, the MR-S roadster is yet another back-to-basics open two-seater with handling benefiting, like its predecessor, from the presence of a mid-located engine.

LIKE MANY other successful performance cars, this model began life as a concept car that Toyota unveiled at the 1997 Tokyo Motor Show. Stripped to its essentials, the silver MR-S was, at 12ft 6in (3810mm) long, over a foot (305mm) shorter than the current MR2. Unlike in that model, the presence of the mid-located engine was less apparent with cooling ducts discreetly tucked in behind the doors. They contrasted with the obvious twin ducting of the MR2.

The show car's engine was a new lightweight four-cylinder 1.8 litre unit with variable valve timing which changes its characteristics to give more power and torque at low speeds, with a consequent improvement in petrol consumption.

The essentials of the concept car have been carried over to the production version which will be called the MR-Spyder. Styling is the work of Toyota's own design studio and the front of the MR-S has been mildly reworked with smaller air scoops and similar detail changes made at the rear.

Likewise the transversely located 1.8 litre power unit, with five valves per cylinder, has been retained, the 170bhp unit endowing the 1984lb (900kg) car with a 0-60mph (97km/h) figure below the seven second mark. A 200bhp version with the engine from Toyota's latest Celica sports coupe also seems likely.

The specification of the interior has been scaled down from that of the concept car with the aluminium finishes of the dashboard replaced by more conventional plastic material. But the distinctive roll-over hoops behind the front seats have disappeared. There is space for luggage at the rear of the cockpit, stowage always being a problem with a mid-engined car.

On the show vehicle the gearlever sprang from a handsome aluminium gate and a sequential gearbox was employed. Gear changes could be made in a conventional manner or racing-style by buttons mounted on the steering wheel, thus allowing drivers to keep both hands on the wheel at all times.

Steering is an electric/hydraulic design which permits driver responsiveness but has the advantage of being lighter than the conventional type.

The car's steel substructure is more conventional with its own purpose-designed platform. The panels are bolt-on units, the idea

being that owners can easily remove them and fit lighter carbon fibre ones in their place.

The all-round strut suspension reflects Toyota's rallying experience and it has the advantage of being lighter than a wishbone layout. Weight is inevitably an ever-present consideration in the development of this no-frills, fun roadster.

With the MR-S Toyota hopes to recapture some of the market share lost to rivals such as Mazda's acclaimed front-engine/rear-drive MX-5. Supplies are expected to reach Britain by the year 2000 with the MR-S's no-nonsense specifications being reflected by prices below the £20,000 mark.

SPECIFICATION	TOYOTA MR-S
Engine location	Front, in-line
Configuration	4-cylinder
Bore and stroke	Not available
Capacity	1800cc
Valve operation	Twin overhead camshafts, 4 valves per cylinder
Horsepower	140bhp @ 6400rpm
Transmission	Five speed
Drive	Rear
Chassis	Unitary
Suspension – front	MacPherson strut
Suspension – rear	MacPherson strut
Brakes	Disc
Top speed	130mph (209km/h)
Acceleration	0-60mph (0-97km/h) 6.5 seconds

BRITAIN: FAST, FURIOUS AND FUN

 *Britain, traditional home of the open sports car, continues to produce an extraordinary variety of performance models although its motor industry is now almost exclusively in the hands of overseas owners.*

JAGUAR, ARGUABLY the country's most famous sporting make, has since 1989 been owned by Ford and the first car to be built under its aegis was the potent XK8 of 1996.

With its origins reaching back to the memorable SS sports cars of the 1930s, Jaguar, as the company became in 1945, is forever remembered for its five wins at Le Mans in the 1950s, for the fast, stylish XK family and, above all, for its sensational E-Type built between 1961 and 1974.

Ford has, since 1987, also owned Aston Martin, a company that has been making sports cars since 1922. Best remembered in its recent history for the famous DB series cars of the 1960s, the famous prefix was recently revived for the acclaimed DB7 coupe of 1993. Thus reinvigorated, Aston Martin now has a second line in a model portfolio headed by the fearsome Vantage V8 600.

This is powered by the company's own V8 engine, but a Ford unit of that configuration is widely employed by British manufacturers of performance cars. It was used to power AC's Anglo/American Cobra of 1962–69 vintage and is currently to be found under the bonnets of the open two-seater Ace and its Aceca coupe stablemate.

Similarly, a revived Jensen's S-V8 is Ford V8-powered. For a firm best remembered for its Interceptor grand tourer, this two-seater roadster represents a move into a new market sector. Happily Jensen is British-owned and the same goes for Marcos, a make born in 1959. It is V8-powered although the new MantaRay also uses a Rover unit.

All these are of American origin but Dare DZ's four-cylinder twin-cam is the Ford engine created for its Mondeo saloon. The cheeky two-seater DZ coupe is produced by the Walklett brothers, co-founders of the Ginetta marque, which dates from 1957.

One of the Ginetta's great contemporaries was the potent, sure-footed Mini Cooper of 1961. Although discontinued ten years later, the concept was revived in 1990 by the Rover Group, which still builds the standard Mini, and the Cooper is once again

commonplace on Britain's roads. Rover, owned since 1994 by BMW, is also custodian of the MG marque, which dates from 1924. In the post-war years its T Series Midgets, MGA and MGB were the most popular British sports cars to be sold in America and although the B ceased production in 1980, the make was revived after a 15-year hiatus in 1995 with the arrival of the acclaimed mid-engined MGF roadster.

It is powered by Rover's own K Series engine and this unit is also used in the similarly configured Lotus Elise. This is a latter-day statement of the no-frills but thrills-aplenty Lotus Seven of 1957 that was followed by the gorgeous but noisy Elite coupe. No longer British owned, in 1996 Lotus was bought by the Malaysian Proton company.

The versatile Rover K four also powers the stark but deceptively sophisticated Westfield FW 400 of 1998. It is based on a light but costly carbon-fibre substructure and this material is extensively featured in the sensational McLaren F1 coupe of 1993. Although production ceased in 1997, its top speed of close on 240mph (386km/h) still makes it the world's fastest road car.

Designed by Gordon Murray, this engineer also played a key role in the creation of that memorable racer for the road, the Rocket, that outwardly has more in common with a 1950s Formula 1 single-seater than the 1990s.

One British sports car that has been effectively reborn in the last decade of this century is the now thriving TVR company. Owned since 1981 by Peter Wheeler, this sports car maker is fortunate that its proprietor is also a supremely talented stylist who has not only completely transformed the Blackpool-built car's appearance, but also its mechanical integrity. TVR's are now powered by their own engines.

Wheeler made his money as an oil industry chemist and, coincidentally, Klaas Zwart, who created the new 200mph (322km/h) Ascari Ecosse coupe, also made his fortune servicing this North Sea enterprise. In these two instances at least, this relatively new industry has lubricated the wheels of an older but still buoyant one!

Above: The AC Ace which paved the way for the Cobra. This is a 1955 example.

Left: Aston Martin's famous DB6 with its distinctive rear spoiler in powerful Vantage guise. Top speed is 148mph (238km/h).

Right: Master of innovations, Lotus's Elite was the world's first glass-fibre monocoque. Produced in the 1958–63 era, it was the company's first significant road car.

AC Aceca

Established in 1903, AC is one of Britain's oldest surviving car makers. The first Aceca appeared in 1928. The name was revived in 1954 and ascribed to a coupe version of the open two-seater Ace, so it is wholly appropriate that the latest car to carry the name maintains this tradition.

Above: Able to carry four people – AC says that taller individuals can be accommodated in the back of the Aceca.

Below: It is 9.8 inches (250mm) longer than the open-two seater Ace.

I T IS based on the two-seater Ace roadster, launched in 1993. Styled by International Automotive Design of Worthing, Sussex, it was powered by a 240bhp 4.9 litre Ford V8, and built up around a substantial stainless steel substructure clad with aluminium body panels. Suspension was all-independent and top speed in excess of 140mph (225km/h).

The Ace entered production in 1994, but two years later the business went into receivership and it was bought in 1996 by the Pride Automotive Group, headed by Alan Lubinsky. Under the direction of general manager Jan-Erik Jansson, formerly of Volvo, the Ace was re-engineered and the revised model unveiled at the 1997 London Motor Show.

It outwardly differed from the formative version by being offered with a substantial hardtop. Changes were made to the front of the car that was now distinguished by the presence of rectangular head lamps, which replaced the twin units, and there was a new mesh-effect grille.

But many more changes were made below the surface. Engine output was boosted to 310bhp and the chassis structure was re-engineered to reduce its weight by some 20 per cent. The front and rear subframes were lightened and stiffened, the original 16in (406mm) wheels replaced by 17in (432 mm) ones and the interior remodelled. The revived Ace was followed by the Aceca coupe that was launched at the 1998 British Motor Show. Benefiting from 9.8in (250mm) being added to the roadster's chassis, its front-end styling was essentially the same, while the coupe body came complete with tailgate.

But unlike the Ace, the Aceca is powered by Ford's 325bhp four-camshaft V8 used in the Ford Mustang, the same power unit employed in the Jensen S-V8 (see pages 70–71). This engine was extended to the Ace in the Spring of 1999.

Priced at close on £70,000, the Aceca offers performance combined with refinement, plus the individuality associated with a specialist manufacturer. AC's premises are, appropriately, located within the boundaries of the old Brooklands motor racing circuit where its cars scored many triumphs in the 1920s.

SPECIFICATION	AC ACECA
Engine location	Front, in-line
Configuration	V8
Bore and stroke	90 x 90mm
Capacity	4601cc
Valve operation	Twin overhead camshafts, 4 valves per cylinder
Horsepower	320bhp @ 5800rpm
Transmission	Five speed
Drive	Rear
Chassis	Unitary
Suspension – front	Wishbone and coil springs
Suspension – rear	Wishbone and coil springs
Brakes	Ventilated disc
Top speed	155mph (249km/h)
Acceleration	0-60mph (0-97km/h) 6.1 seconds

Ascari Ecosse

The exclusive 200mph (322km/h) club has recently recruited a new member with the arrival, in 1999, of the shapely contours of the BMW-engined Ascari Ecosse coupe.

The sense of wellbeing engendered by the Ascari's luxurious interior is enhanced by the use of hand-stitched leather upholstery.

THE MAN behind the car is Klaas Zwart, a self-made Dutch tycoon, who in 1980 began to develop specialist tools for the Scottish oil and gas industry in the garden shed of his home near Aberdeen. Today, nearly 20 years on, turnover has reached £21 million and the company has eight offices throughout the world.

A motoring racing enthusiast and driver, Zwart was an active participant in Grand Touring competition and it was there that he encountered the Ascari FGT sports racer designed by Lee Noble.

This used a traditional tubular space-frame chassis, boxed with aluminium, cloaked by an attractive and distinctive glass-fibre coupe body. Power came from a big 5.7 litre pushrod Ford V8.

The Dutchman was so impressed with the car – it had a good year on the circuits in 1995 – that he bought the business in 1996 and launched the Ascari FGT for public sale. But the competition car made an uneasy transition to the road and Zwart decided, instead, to use it as a starting point from which to develop the Ecosse. Launched at the 1998 British Motor Show and priced at £89,000, it entered production in 1999.

At the heart of the mid-engined coupe is a Hartge-tuned 4.7 litre BMW V8 engine that develops no less than 400bhp at 6100rpm. This location permits a well-balanced front/rear 47/53 percentage split.

The coupe body contributes to a dry weight of 2755lb (1250kg) resulting in a claimed blistering 0-60mph (97km/h) time of 4.1 seconds and 200mph (322km/h) top speed. This is faster than the FGT that could attain 175mph (282km/h).

Ascari Cars, based in Blandford, Dorset, has, at the time of writing, 10 employees, one for every car so far built. Customers can specify their personal preferences as far as colour and interior trim are concerned, and the company claims the car has 'more pulling power...in every sense!'

Top and above: The mid-engined, glass-fibre-bodied Ascari is powered by a tuned BMW V8 engine and has a racing pedigree.

SPECIFICATION	ASCARI ECOSSE
Engine location	Mid, in-line
Configuration	V8
Bore and stroke	92 x 88mm
Capacity	4700cc
Valve operation	Twin overhead camshafts, 4 valves per cylinder
Horsepower	400bhp @ 6100rpm
Transmission	Five speed
Drive	Rear
Chassis	Tubular space-frame
Suspension – front	Wishbones and coil springs
Suspension – rear	Wishbones and coil springs
Brakes	Ventilated disc
Top speed	200mph (322km/h)
Acceleration	0-60mph (0-97km/h) 4.1 seconds

Aston Martin Vantage V8 600

With a top speed in excess of 200mph (322km/h), the Aston Martin Vantage is currently Britain's fastest production car. Handbuilt at the company's Newport Pagnell factory, and priced at £190,000, it is also the most expensive.

The 5.3 litre V8 with twin Eaton superchargers. Each now has its own intercooled radiator and water pump.

THE ORIGINS of this latest version are rooted in the Vantage announced in 1992. Since 1950 this name has been intermittently applied to the most powerful Aston Martin of its day. The new car was the culmination of extensive testing, that lasted for over a year, at the hands of former world champion Jackie Stewart.

Based on Aston Martin's lacklustre Virage coupe of 1990, it was extensively reworked; the Vantage is lower, wider but heavier than the model on which it was based.

But the principal differences are mechanical and, of these, the fitment of two Eaton superchargers to the company's long-running but still formidable 5.3 litre 32-valve V8 engine is the most significant. The standard Virage developed some 330bhp but these ministrations resulted in a 70 per cent increase in power to no less than 550bhp, making the unit one of the most powerful production engines of its day.

Such stupendous performance required modifications to the car's brakes and the 14in (356mm) diameter discs were the largest units then fitted to a production car. The front callipers had been transferred *in toto* from Aston Martin's Group C sports racer. Their installation was demanded by the fact that the Vantage could reach 0-62mph (100km/h) in just 4.6 seconds, 100mph (161km/h) in 10.1, while top speed was nudging 190mph (306km/h). A close-ratio six-speed ZF gearbox was fitted although a three-speed automatic was available as an option.

In mid-1995 came a Mark II version of the design which incorporated no less than 700 improvements, although the only apparent outward differences were a new crackle-finish radiator grille and the provision of fog and reversing lights.

Mechanical modifications were largely concerned with refining the engine, which still produces the same power, and to handling, gear change and interior noise levels. Performance otherwise remained the same.

Impressive as the eye-watering performance is, Aston Martin has not rested on its laurels and for the 1999 season introduced an

Left: The 10 per cent increase in engine output has required improvements to the Vantage's steering, suspension and brakes, the latter being special ventilated and grooved racing units.

Right: A 600 in its element! What Aston Martin calls a V8 Driving Dynamics package is available on both new and existing Vantages. It comes in response to customer comments over a two-year period.

even more powerful 600bhp version of the Vantage which, if customers want to stump up £43,000, will result in their cars being so updated.

Modifications include the introduction of an intercooled radiator and water pump to each supercharger which have the effect of reducing the intake charge temperature. Blower output is also increased. A special five-speed gearbox is also available and this, along with a revised rear axle ratio, means that the Vantage can now reach 60mph (97km/h) in under four seconds and 100mph (161km/h) in less than 10. Improvements have been made to braking; there are adjustable shock absorbers and new lighter magnesium wheels.

The Vantage is now capable of speeds in excess of 200mph (322km/h), so making it one of the world's fastest and more desirable supercars.

SPECIFICATION	ASTON MARTIN VANTAGE V8 600
Engine location	Front, in-line
Configuration	V8, twin supercharged
Bore and stroke	100 x 85mm
Capacity	5340cc
Valve operation	Twin overhead camshafts, 4 valves per cylinder
Horsepower	600bhp @ 6750rpm
Transmission	Six speed
Drive	Rear
Chassis	Unitary
Suspension – front	Wishbones and coil springs
Suspension – rear	Wishbones and coil springs
Brakes	Ventilated disc
Top speed	Over 200mph (322km/h)
Acceleration	0-60mph (0-97km/h) 3.9 seconds

Bentley Hunaudières

If enough people want one, this 200mph (322km/h) Bentley four-wheel-drive supercar could be in production by 2001. Unveiled as a concept car to the surprise of the public and press at the 1999 Geneva Motor Show, it marks the first tangible display of Volkswagen's ownership of this legendary, hitherto British-owned, marque.

IN TRUTH the concept was already in existence prior to the VW takeover, but the idea immediately chimed with chairman Ferdinand Piech, grandson of Ferdinand Porsche, who had, when working for the family firm, created the mighty 917 which gave Porsche its first Le Mans victory in 1970. Created by German and British engineers at Volkswagen's Wolfsburg prototype facility, the one-off show car was based on the substructure of a Lamborghini Diablo. VW also bought that company in 1998.

At this coupe's heart is a new mid-located 8 litre 623bhp V16 engine, with no less than 64 valves, a derivative of the WR12 unit that the German company unveiled in 1997. But convention has been abandoned, and instead of two banks of eight cylinders in line, paired blocks of four are staggered so the resulting engine is as compact as a V8. A five-speed automatic gearbox is employed and the interior features leather and mottled aluminium that echoes the style of the 1920s.

And that unusual name? It comes from the Les Hunaudières straight on the Le Mans circuit where the big green Bentleys won in 1924 and successively from 1927 until 1931. Could history repeat itself? This sleek coupe is finished in a racing green livery...

SPECIFICATION	BENTLEY HUNAUDIÈRES
Engine location	Mid, longitudinal
Configuration	V16
Bore and stroke	84 x 90mm
Capacity	8004cc
Valve operation	Twin overhead camshafts, 4 valves per cylinder
Horsepower	623bhp @ 6000rpm
Transmission	Five speed automatic
Drive	Four wheel
Chassis	Tubular steel
Suspension – front	Wishbones and coil springs
Suspension – rear	Wishbones and coil springs
Brakes	Ventilated disc
Top speed	200mph (322km/h)
Acceleration	0-60mph (0-97km/h) 4 seconds

Big, brutal and a Bentley, the Hunaudières' pedigree is underlined by the time-honoured wire-mesh front grille. Power comes from a mid-located V16 engine and handling is enhanced by ride and pitch control, compliant suspension and large wheels shod with low profile tyres. It received a mixed reception at its '99 Geneva launch.

Mini Cooper

You can't keep a good car down! Although the three times Monte Carlo Rally-winning model was axed in 1971, no less than 19 years later it was revived, and it will remain in production until the seemingly evergreen Mini makes way in the year 2000 for its similarly named successor.

Above: Incredibly the roots of the Mini's Cooper 1275cc engine reach back to 1951!
Below: The bonnet stripes, fog lamps and wheels differentiate the Cooper from the mainstream version.

THE BRAINCHILD of John Cooper, whose Cooper Car Company had won the Formula 1 constructors' championships in 1959 and 1960, the original 997cc Mini Cooper was launched in 1961. Top speed was 85mph (137km/h), some 15mph (24km/h) faster than the standard car, and it enjoyed the good roadholding attributes characteristic of front-wheel-drive.

This in turn paved the way for the more potent 1275cc Cooper S and it was this version that triumphed in the 1964, 1965 and 1967 Monte Carlo events.

But in 1968 the British Motor Corporation, which built the Mini, was taken over by the Leyland car and lorry group. The resulting British Leyland management team decided to axe royalty payments to outside consultants, and the Mini Cooper was a victim of this corporate purge.

However, John Cooper, the car's creator, never lost his belief in the model, and in 1985 he began to export Minis, complete with boxed Cooper conversion kits, to a receptive Japanese market.

This lead the Rover Group to revive the model, and in 1990 it prefaced its reintroduction with a limited edition of 1000 cars with the distinctive white roof that had featured on some examples, and now adorned with white bonnet stripes that bore John Cooper's signature.

Powered by a 1275cc descendant of the long-running A Series engine used in the original car, output was boosted to 61bhp which gave it a top speed of 85mph (137km/h). This was about the same as the original car, but the new model was quieter than the '60s versions!

Despite the passage of years, it's still a bit special, and this explains why the basic car has happily reached its 40th birthday although the Mini name will live on into the 21st century. Its front-wheel-drive/transverse engine layout has truly changed the course of car design the world over.

SPECIFICATION	MINI COOPER
Engine location	Front, transverse
Configuration	4-cylinder
Bore and stroke	70 x 81mm
Capacity	1275cc
Valve operation	Pushrod
Horsepower	63bhp @ 5500rpm
Transmission	Four speed
Drive	Front
Chassis	Unitary
Suspension – front	Wishbones and cone
Suspension – rear	Trailing arms, coil springs
Brakes	Front disc, rear drum
Top speed	85mph (137km/h)
Acceleration	0-60mph (0-97km/h) 13.5 seconds

Dare DZ

This is a car that would look at home being driven by the comic-strip space hero, Dan Dare, Pilot of the Future. But Dare in this instance stands for Design and Research Engineering and space in the snug cockpit is at something of a premium!

The Dare's interior is well finished with leather seats and carpeting, while the distinctive aluminium kickplate aids entry and exit.

THE MID-engined DZ is a first cousin once removed of the Ginetta sports car, built since 1957 by the four Walklett brothers. After 32 years they disposed of the business in 1989 and production was transferred from Witham, Essex to Scunthorpe, Humberside.

Then, in 1991, two of the Ginetta founding team, Trevers and Ivor Walklett, and Trevers' son Mark, established Dare as an Essex-based engineering consultancy. But the ensuing recession forced Ginetta briefly into receivership in 1992, to the dismay of Tamotsu Maeda, its Japanese importers, which earlier in the year had acquired the manufacturing and sales rights, badges and names for the classic Ginetta G4 and its mid-engined G12 coupe derivative.

Because of demand for the cars in the Far East, Maeda then contracted Dare to produce these cars which it subsequently re-engineered. Production restarted at a new manufacturing facility established by the Walkletts in Colchester, Essex.

Funding from this contract has provided the £500,000 development costs to get the Dare DZ, unveiled at the 1998 British Motor Show, into production alongside the G4 and G12.

Based on a tubular-steel chassis with all-independent wishbone and coil-sprung suspension, the exposed arms are chromed, racing style, which is wholly in keeping with the car's competition-related appearance. The glass-fibre-bodied coupe, with its distinctive gullwing doors, ensures that the Dare is like nothing else on the road with the exception of the Light Car Company's 1992 Rocket described on pages 78–79.

The lines are those of a two-seater racing car, with aerofoils front and rear, but equipped for the road with front cycle wings and headlamps.

The DZ initials stand for Dare Zetec, the latter name reflecting the choice of Ford's twin-cam Zetec saloon car engines. There is an 130bhp 2 litre naturally aspirated version, and a 210bhp supercharged top-line four of the same capacity comes later.

Even in unblown form the mid-positioned, transversely mounted twin-cam will propel the 1499lb (680kg) car to 130mph (209km/h) with 60mph (97km/h) whistling up in an impressive 5.8 seconds from a standing start.

The interior is sumptuously appointed, but as the car, like the two Ginettas, is destined principally for Japanese customers, its dimensions are tailored for their slighter frames. However, work is already underway on a longer-wheelbase open version that will be more suited for lankier British buyers. The leather upholstery and

SPECIFICATION	DARE DZ
Engine location	Mid, transverse
Configuration	4-cylinder
Bore and stroke	85 x 88mm
Capacity	1996cc
Valve operation	Twin overhead camshafts, 4 valves per cylinder
Horsepower	130bhp @ 5700rpm
Transmission	Five speed
Drive	Rear
Chassis	Multi tubular steel
Suspension – front	Wishbones and coil springs
Suspension – rear	Wishbones and coil springs
Brakes	Ventilated disc
Top speed	130mph (209km/h)
Acceleration	0-60mph (0-97km/h) 5.4 seconds

carpeting are in stark contrast to the likes of the more spartan Lotus Elise or Caterham Seven. Head restraints carry the Dare logo and the machined aluminium kickplate is a nice touch.

The Walkletts hope to sell about half of the projected 100 cars a year they intend to build in the UK. Why not, as they say, 'Dare to Be Different.'

Above: The alternative convertible version of the DZ. Owners can thus enjoy the pleasures of open-air motoring although carrying capacity is less than the coupe's. Note the exposed front suspension and that different pattern alloy wheels are fitted. In both versions the rears are wider than the fronts.

Above: The daringly styled DZ outwardly resembles a racing car, if one was made in two-seater coupe form! The front wing and rear spoiler underline this inspiration while the doors open gull-wing style. The Dare is popular in Japan and is also available on the UK market.

Jaguar XK8

Jaguar's famous sporting line was revived in 1996 with the arrival of the XK8, a 155mph (249km/h) car powered by an impressive new 4 litre V8 engine.

Jaguar's first V8 appeared in the aptly named XK8. It is also produced in supercharged form.

THE LAUNCH, at that year's Geneva Motor Show, was timed to coincide with the 35th anniversary of the unveiling of the company's famous E-Type there back in 1961. But while that model was destined to be Jaguar's most famous sports car, the two-plus-two XK8 is more expensive and well-appointed to compete in a market exemplified by the Mercedes-Benz SL (see page 22).

Work on the project, coded X100, began in 1992. The starting point of the new Jaguar was its XJS predecessor's floorpan and ancillaries clothed in distinctive coupe and roadster bodies essayed by chief stylist Geoff Lawson. Although thoroughly modern in

execution, there are echoes of the E-Type and of the company's XJ13 mid-engined sports racer, built for the Le Mans 24 hour race in the 1960s but never run there.

But this was much more than a purely cosmetic enhancement. More significantly, beneath the long, graceful bonnet is a completely new V8 engine, only the fourth power unit in Jaguar's history. Considerable relief was expressed by commentators and public alike that Ford, Jaguar's owners since 1989, had not attempted to foist one of its V8s on the Coventry company. Instead the marque's integrity has remained intact because the XK8 unit,

Above: The spirit of the E-Type is recaptured in the XK8 convertible that has established itself as a worthy successor.

Right: The competition-style grille and bonnet louvres indicate this is the supercharged XKR version, also available in open guise.

soon extended to the XJ saloon range, was designed by Jaguar engineers and is only used in its cars.

The 4 litre alloy unit is the company's first V8 and, with twin overhead camshafts per cylinder bank, it is more compact and powerful than the six-cylinder engine it replaced.

The *8* in the car's name thus refers to the new power unit while the *XK* prefix is used in tribute to the company's legendary XK twin-overhead-camshaft engine that powered every Jaguar between 1950 and 1971 and survived until 1992. And the fact that the E-Type was known as the XKE in the all-important American market was a further reason for its use.

With the emphasis firmly placed on refinement, a five-speed automatic gearbox was specified, although a manual unit is promised for the future.

Since the Second World War America has been Jaguar's most important market and some 80 per cent of XK8s have crossed the Atlantic. The open version has proved to be the most popular of the two body options.

In 1998 came the more potent XKR version which uses the supercharged V8 first used in the XJR saloon of the previous year. Outwardly identifiable by a competition-like mesh grille and bonnet louvres, the blown six develops 363bhp – 73 more than the

SPECIFICATION	JAGUAR XK8
Engine location	Front, in-line
Configuration	V8
Bore and stroke	86 x 86mm
Capacity	3995cc
Valve operation	Twin overhead camshafts, 4 valves per cylinder
Horsepower	290bhp @ 6100rpm
Transmission	Five speed automatic
Drive	Rear
Chassis	Unitary
Suspension – front	Wishbones and coil springs
Suspension – rear	Wishbones and coil springs
Brakes	Ventilated disc
Top speed	155mph (249km/h)
Acceleration	0-60mph (0-97km/h) 6.6 seconds

standard version. Although the limited 155mph (249km/h) top speed remains the same, the 0-60mph (97km/h) figure is reduced to 5.2 seconds, making it 1.4 seconds quicker.

Thus reinvigorated, Jaguar looks set to hold its own in a world market that becomes more competitive by the year. The big cat is definitely back!

Jensen S-V8

The big, chunky Jensen, in production again in 1999 after a seven-year absence, is powered by an American Ford V8 engine, just like the first of the breed which dates from 1936.

IN 1997 the Jensen name was bought by the auto development company, Creative, of Redditch, Worcestershire, run by Keith Rauer and Robin Bowyer. Their business specializes in developing concepts for the motor industry and, having turned ideas into experimental cars for other companies, they reckoned that the time had come to undertake a similar exercise for themselves.

Rauer and Bowyer identified what they perceived to be a gap in the market, that could be filled by a traditional British open two-seater, between the bastions of TVR on one hand and Porsche on the other. The brains behind the new car are ex-Jaguar engineers Howard Guy and Gary Doy, who did not join Creative as employees but instead established their own company, Design Q, on its premises. It took 18 months to progress from concept stage to the unveiling of the prototype at the 1998 British Motor Show and the car entered production in the latter half of 1999. Creative has a distinct advantage of having a tool-making facility and can produce its own pressed-aluminium panels.

The last Jensen, the Interceptor of 1967–76, briefly revived in 1983–92, was a two-plus-two coupe but the new car radically differs from it. With the emphasis on performance, the new S-V8, the *S* stands for Sport, is an uncompromising two-seater, aluminium-bodied roadster. Nevertheless, its distinctive styling echoes some of the famous Jensens of the past. The twin sloping headlamps are reminiscent of the Jensen CV8 of the 1962–66 era and there are echoes of the Interceptor and the Jensen-Healey sports car.

The body is mounted on a perimeter frame chassis with all-independent wishbones and coil springs front and rear. The traditional in-line engine and rear-drive layout is maintained and although the prototype used the 325bhp, four-cam, 4.6 litre V8 that powers Ford's Mustang, the production version will employ a 350bhp version of the same unit. The five-speed manual gearbox comes from the same source. Top speed is limited to 150mph (249km/h).

The black-finished interior is handsome, distinctive and professionally finished, with polished aluminium alloy used to

Above: The S-V8's distinctive rear with twin exhausts suggestive of V8 power.

Right: Unlike past Jensens, this is a two-seater sports car, but frontal styling echoes the CV8 of the 1960s. This prototype has a plastic body but production versions will be aluminium.

good effect in the central console and on the gearlever knob. Steering, by rack and pinion, is power-assisted and a mere 2.8 turns are required to go from lock to lock.

It is intended to sell this new Jensen at around £40,000 and Creative's aim is initially to produce the S-V8 at the rate of 300 a year at its Redditch premises. If demands warrants it, output would then be transferred to a new factory in the vicinity. The eventual aim is to build about 600 cars annually.

Only the state of the world economy and the demands of the marketplace will determine whether this attempt to revive a respected marque will succeed. If it does, the minuscule British-owned motor industry will be one more make to the good.

SPECIFICATION	JENSEN S-V8
Engine location	Front, in-line
Configuration	V8
Bore and stroke	90 x 90mm
Capacity	4601cc
Valve operation	Twin overhead camshafts, 4 valves per cylinder
Horsepower	325bhp @ 5800rpm
Transmission	Five speed
Drive	Rear
Chassis	Unitary
Suspension – front	Wishbones and coil springs
Suspension – rear	Wishbones and coil springs
Brakes	Ventilated disc
Top speed	150mph (241km/h)
Acceleration	0-60mph (0-97km/h) 4.9 seconds

Right: The attention to detail is impressive and the 'gills,' just ahead of the leading edges of both doors, are particularly noteworthy. Bodywork is produced in-house.

Lotus 340R

When Lotus launched the mid-engined Elise in 1995, it was a clear restatement of its spartan but potent Seven model of the 1950s. Well-received by the public and press alike, the company, in conjunction with Autocar magazine, then took the concept one stage further.

Above: The 340R's doorless, no-frills cockpit; some protection is offered by the high sides. The Alcantara-trimmed steering wheel is removable to improve access.

THE RESULT is the lightened, more powerful and faster 340R that was unveiled at the 1998 British Motor Show. One of the Elise's innovative features was its extruded aluminium chassis, and while this is retained intact, some composite body panels have been added which has had the effect of noticeably changing the car's appearance. These are all detachable and there are smaller panels at the front and rear that can be removed so that the owner can check hydraulic fluid and the engine's oil and water levels.

Although it remains a two-seater, the revised bodywork is suggestive of a single-seater racer, although the two roll-over hoops are the give-away. There are, unsurprisingly, no doors!

The wheels and all-independent suspension are open to view although embryo mudguards are fitted. The wheels are very light OZ F1 centre-lock units, at the back are enlarged 17-inch (431mm) wheels, while the fronts, by contrast, are 16-inch (406mm).

The nose, complete with mesh grille, reflects the Elise's Seven ancestry and extends well forward of the projector beam headlamps that emit light through elongated slits in the bodywork.

From the back the 340R is naked and unashamed with its drive shafts and rear suspension open to view. There is a bespoke chrome exhaust system with its silencer contained within a circular envelope of carbon fibre. Which bring us to the engine.

The standard Elise is powered by the 1.8 litre, Rover K Series, twin-cam four that is essentially the same unit that powers the MGF. In its standard 118bhp form, it gives the mainstream model a 120mph (177km/h) plus top speed. But the intention is to fit this so-called super Elise with a more potent 170bhp version of the K, although the show car sported the mainstream Elise unit.

The wishbone suspension is essentially standard but there is an uprated front anti-roll bar and stronger shock absorbers. Brakes are similarly improved and employ four-pot racing calipers.

Once seated in the car, the driver will notice that the dashboard has been removed, and the speedometer and tachometer are mounted either side and above the removable steering wheel. There is a string of control buttons where you might expect to find a central console. Racing seats, complete with five-point harnesses, are fitted and some crash protection is offered by the high-sided doorless cockpit.

The standard Elise turns the scales at a respectable 1488lb (675kg) but the 340 only weighs 1102lb (500kg) and has a claimed 133mph (214km/h) top speed, a good 10mph (16km/h) more than the standard Elise. Acceleration is similarly enhanced.

As a result of its enthusiastic thumbs-up at the car's show debut, this minimalist Elise is to enter production in 1999. The spirit of the original Lotus Seven lives on, with a vengeance!

SPECIFICATION	LOTUS 340R
Engine location	Mid, transverse
Configuration	4-cylinder
Bore and stroke	80 x 89mm
Capacity	1796cc
Valve operation	Twin overhead camshafts, 4 valves per cylinder
Horsepower	170bhp @ 8000rpm
Transmission	Five speed
Drive	Rear
Chassis	Extruded aluminium
Suspension – front	Wishbones and coil springs
Suspension – rear	Wishbones and coil springs
Brakes	Ventilated disc
Top speed	133mph (214km/h)
Acceleration	0-60mph (0-97km/h) 4 seconds

Left: The 340R is lighter and more powerful than the standard Elise, and it looks like nothing else on the road. The roll-over bars contribute an air of purpose and style. Wheels are shod with handcut Yokohama slicks.

Below: Naked and unashamed: the 340R's rear suspension and twin stainless-steel tail pipes that exit either side of the silencer are exposed to view. Note the car's name proclaimed beneath. The Lotus engineers' intention was to attain 340bhp per tonne.

McLaren F1

Although the last F1 was completed at the end of 1997, it still stands supreme as the world's fastest and most sophisticated road car being capable of over 230mph (370km/h).

CREATED BY McLaren, eight times winner of the Formula 1 constructors' championship, the F1 was the brainchild of its technical director, Gordon Murray. With such a pedigree it was inevitable that this distinctive coupe would be a racer at heart.

Styling was the work of Peter Stevens who already had the sports racing XJR-15 Jaguar and the latter-day Lotus Elan to his credit. The intention was to build 300 cars, but such a machine would not come cheap and in the event each F1 retailed for no less than £530,000 apiece. Ultra-light but costly carbon fibre featured extensively, and the substructure incorporated no less than 94 pieces of the material used in conjunction with an aluminium and honeycomb-structured Nomex core.

Power came from a mid-located, longitudinally mounted, 6.1 litre 627bhp V12 engine designed especially for the F1 by BMW

Motorsport and unrelated to the similarly configured unit used in the German company's 7 Series road cars. Drive was conveyed to the rear wheels, not as might be expected to all four, via a six-speed gearbox.

This formidable package was clothed in an aerodynamically honed coupe body made, like the substructure, of carbon fibre. It featured ingenious doors that opened both forwards and upwards.

The air-conditioned cockpit was designed for three individuals. The driver, who sat well to the fore, was unusually positioned in the centre in a seat upholstered in startling red leather. The passengers' seats, by contrast, were black. Starting was effected by the driver first raising a dashboard flap and then pressing a large red button!

As the F1 was designed for speeds well in excess of 200mph (322km/h), its underside had been designed to harness 'ground effect', a concept usually reserved for racing cars that helps a car adhere to the road. It was also fitted with two fans to remove the so-called boundary air that would otherwise have made the coupe tail-light.

The first F1 was delivered in January 1994 but, as production numbers crept up, McLaren recognized that it could be homologated (i.e. approved) for racing. The outcome was the GTR version that, shorn of its roadgoing refinements, was lighter, and developed a restricted 636bhp. It went on to triumph in the 1995 GT Championship and again in the following year's series.

As if this was not enough, it also won Le Mans first time out in 1995, with other F1s coming in third, fourth, fifth and thirteenth positions. It was the first instance since the 1940s that the 24 hour race had been won by a road car but, as must be apparent, this was no ordinary street machine!

To commemorate this success, later in 1995 McLaren built five orange-painted versions of the racer, appropriately titled the LM. Perversely, these road cars were even more powerful and produced 668bhp, even if gearing restricted the top speed to a mere 220mph (354km/h)...

Finally, in 1997, came the F1 GT, the ultimate roadgoer, longer and wider than the original and fitted with a rear wing to help keep downforce in check. Created to challenge the ultimately successful Porsche 911-based GT1, just eight were built.

But F1 sales never reached their expected levels. It took a month to produce between one and two cars and production ceased late in 1997. By this time the F1's price had risen to £634,500 and, in the end, just 100 examples of this extraordinary vehicle were built. Only 10 found British buyers, the remaining 90 were sold abroad.

Left: The F1's scissor doors displayed to effect. Note the central steering wheel; this McLaren can carry three, a driver and two passengers.

Above: McLaren's 1995 Le Mans winner – a still dust-bespattered F1 GTR at that year's Goodwood Festival of Speed.

SPECIFICATION	McLAREN F1
Engine location	Mid, longitudinal
Configuration	V12
Bore and stroke	86 x 87mm
Capacity	6064cc
Valve operation	Twin overhead camshafts, 4 valves per cylinder
Horsepower	627bhp @ 7400rpm
Transmission	Six speed
Drive	Rear
Chassis	Advanced composite monocoque
Suspension – front	Wishbones and coil springs
Suspension – rear	Wishbones and coil springs
Brakes	Ventilated disc
Top speed	Over 231mph (372km/h)
Acceleration	0-60mph (0-97km/h) 3.2 seconds

Marcos MantaRay

Marcos, which began making its distinctive sports cars in 1959, is one of the British motor industry's great survivors. Created by racing driver Jem Marsh, and aerodynamicist Frank Costin, the name was a combination of their surnames.

The MantaRay combines the appearance of a traditional sports car with the performance and practicality of a current one. Four-cylinder and V8 versions are available.

THE ORIGINAL Marcos hit the headlines because it had a plywood chassis, rather than the customary steel, although this only lasted until 1969. The distinctive lines were the work of stylist Dennis Adams, and these were faithfully retained as the marque evolved, although the mechanicals and interiors were updated.

A long-standing and distinctive feature of the Marcos was its cut-off sloping tail but, courageously, the company has recently decided to make a break with the past and commission a new one. Appropriately the task fell to Leigh Adams, nephew of original stylist Dennis. The result is a softer, flatter look that was first applied to the MantaRay, launched for the 1999 season, which replaced the Mantara that had been in production since 1993.

That model's chassis is carried over, as are the range of existing engines. There are no less than four of these on offer, which gives the MantaRay top speeds varying from 135 to 148mph (217 to 238km/h). There is Rover's four-cylinder, turbocharged, 2 litre unit and 3.9 and 4.6 litre versions of that company's versatile V8.

Top of the range is Ford America's 4.6 litre V8 which powers the glass fibre-bodied car from 0 to 60mph (97km/h) in just 4.8 seconds. Revisions to the tail mean that the model has a capacious

boot, which is further helped by the fact that, unusually, the spare wheel is contained within the bonnet. It also allowed the Wiltshire-based Marcos company to revise the MantaRay's interior which is finished in a traditional combination of wood veneer and leather upholstery. Power steering is fitted as standard.

Available in coupe and spyder forms, this latest Marcos joins a range that consists of the outrageous 165mph (266km/h) Mantis and the Le Mans-bred LM400. Racing does improve the breed!

SPECIFICATION	MARCOS MANTARAY 4.6 V8
Engine location	Front, in-line
Configuration	V8
Bore and stroke	90.2 x 90mm
Capacity	4601cc
Valve operation	Pushrod
Horsepower	280bhp @ 5500rpm
Transmission	Five speed
Drive	Rear
Chassis	Steel space-frame
Suspension – front	MacPherson strut
Suspension – rear	Wishbones and coil springs
Brakes	Ventilated disc
Top speed	148mph (238km/h)
Acceleration	0-60mph (0-97km/h) 4.8 seconds

Left: Visually enhanced by a new tail, this Marcos has a capacious boot because the spare wheel has been ingeniously contained within the bonnet. Steering is adjustable and the mirrors are electrically controlled and heated.

MG*F*

The MG sports car was re-born in 1995 after a 15-year hiatus with the arrival of the acclaimed mid-engined MGF open two-seater. It has the added virtue of being the world's first affordable mid-engined roadster.

Above: The MGF, since 1996 Britain's best-selling sports car. The nose evokes echoes of the MGB.

ITS MGB predecessor ceased production in 1980 and the F was designed during the era when MG's Rover Group parent company was owned by British Aerospace. It was a long time a-coming, work on the project having begun in 1989.

The engine location was partly due to the fact that Mazda's back-to-basics MX-5 sports car had a front engine/rear drive configuration. This was coupled with the fact that an experimental car, coded PR3, was configured in the same way and was much preferred by Rover's directors when pitted against conventional front-engined or front-wheel-drive versions.

Developed in conjunction with the Coventry-based Mayflower, which builds the body, the *F* was styled by Rover's Gerry McGovern and engineered by a team lead by Brian Griffin. But financial constraints meant that the model was not configured for the potentially lucrative American market although, in addition to the UK, this MG is sold throughout the rest of the world, with Japan being its most popular overseas market.

Imbued with the superlative roadholding thanks to the engine position, the *F* is strictly a two-seater. Power comes from Rover's acclaimed 1.8 litre, twin-overhead-camshaft, four-cylinder K Series engine and there are two versions of the design.

The base model develops 118bhp and provides the *F* with a 123mph (198km/h) top speed. But there is also a faster 143bhp VVC model with its power unit enhanced by a variable valve control. This improves torque and top speed, which rises to 130mph (209km/h).

In 1996, the first full year of production, the MGF became Britain's best-selling sports car and remains so at the time of writing (1999.) Thus reinvigorated, the MG marque's future looks bright, despite the much publicized problems afflicting the Rover Group's passenger car line.

Its successor will be engineered for the all-important American market, and then MG really will be motoring.

Above: This is the basic 1.8i model, identifiable by its six-spoke wheels; the VVC version has five spokes.

SPECIFICATION	MGF 1.8i VVC
Engine location	Mid, transverse
Configuration	4-cylinder
Bore and stroke	80 x 89mm
Capacity	1796cc
Valve operation	Twin overhead camshafts, 4 valves per cylinder
Horsepower	143bhp @ 7000rpm
Transmission	Five speed
Drive	Rear
Chassis	Unitary
Suspension – front	Wishbones and coil springs
Suspension – rear	Wishbones and coil springs
Brakes	Disc, ventilated at front
Top speed	130mph (209km/h)
Acceleration	0-60mph (0-97km/h) 7 seconds

Rocket

It looks like a racing car that has mistakenly strayed off the race track and taken to the public road. This is perhaps not surprising, because the Rocket is the work of McLaren's respected technical director, Gordon Murray, whose portfolio includes no less than four world championship-winning single-seaters and the advanced F1 road car.

Above: The 1002cc Yamaha motorcycle engine.
Below: The body is glass fibre, although wings and dashboard are made of carbon fibre.
Right: What the company describes as a one-plus-one!

ANNOUNCED IN 1991, the Rocket entered production in February 1992, although Murray confessed at the time that he had been thinking about the project for nearly 20 years. It had been in 1972, no less, that he and Le Mans driver Chris Craft (who came third in the 1976 event as co-driver of a Lola-Ford) began planning a lightweight road car in the spirit of Colin Chapman's original Lotus Seven.

Built by Craft's Light Car Company of St Neots, Cambridgeshire, Bob Curl was responsible for bringing Murray's and Craft's ideas to production status and he also designed the distinctive body.

The Rocket weighs a mere 775lb (351kg). Every part of the car is purpose designed, and the only proprietary component is its mid-located, four-cylinder, Yamaha FZR twin-cam alloy

SPECIFICATION	ROCKET
Engine location	Mid, transverse
Configuration	4-cylinder
Bore and stroke	76 x 56mm
Capacity	1002cc
Valve operation	Twin overhead camshafts, 5 valves per cylinder
Horsepower	143bhp @ 10,500rpm
Transmission	Five speed
Drive	Rear
Chassis	Space-frame
Suspension – front	Wishbones and coil springs
Suspension – rear	Wishbones and coil springs
Brakes	Front ventilated/drilled disc, rear ventilated disc
Top speed	145mph (233km/h)
Acceleration	0-60mph (0-97km/h) 4.4 seconds

motorcycle engine, with five valves per pot, which powered that company's Genesis two-wheeler.

Had Murray bought in parts, the car would have sold for considerably less than the original £37,000 asking price, but it would have tipped the scales at over 1100lb (499kg), to the detriment of the 145mph (233km/h) top speed and a 0-60mph (97km/h) figure of under five seconds.

Power is conveyed to the rear wheels via a five-speed sequential gearbox. The transaxle, with two alternative final drive ratios, was designed by Peter Weismann of Traction Products in America who has extensive experience of creating transmission systems for Indianapolis cars.

This gives a total of 15 speeds, ten forward and five reverse with changes effected by a racing-style right-hand lever, there being a second shift to engage the different ratios.

It was this extraordinary facility that attracted *Autocar* magazine's Colin Goodwin and in 1998 he succeeded in attaining 101mph (163km/h) in reverse gear down the runway of Kemble airfield in Gloucestershire...

The stove-enamelled space-frame chassis, with stressed light alloy panels coloured to customer order, is clothed with a glass-fibre body inspired by a Vanwall single-seater racer of late 1950s vintage.

As a result, weather protection is non-existent with just a token windshield, but no doors or hood. Carbon-fibre cycle-type wings represent a rare concession to the realities of the road.

As befits its inspiration, this is in reality a single-seater although there is provision for a 'pillion passenger' behind the driver. Created as an out-and-out fun car, it goes like, well, a rocket accompanied by the scream of the 143bhp oversquare short-stroke Yamaha four, which comes complete with roller bearing crankshaft and four carburettors. It is bereft of limiters to permit it to spin fearlessly to 10,500rpm and beyond!

In recent years the Rocket, which is now available with a six-speed 'box, has been built at the LCC's factory in Stanford-in-the-Vale, Oxfordshire with between two and four lucky customers taking delivery each year.

TVR Tuscan

In recent years the TVR company has delighted enthusiasts with a succession of utterly distinctive sports cars that not only have their own carefully crafted persona, but perform just as well as they look.

THE BLACKPOOL-based business once again stole the headlines at the 1998 British Motor Show when it unveiled the new Tuscan roadster, that replaced the Griffith Speed Six which had been introduced at the previous year's London event.

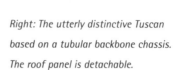

The new Tuscan, that revives a long-standing TVR name, came into being because chairman-cum-chief stylist Peter Wheeler decided that he was not happy about the bonnet of the '97 Six. Working in conjunction with designer Duncan McTaggart, the result is a sleeker but more muscular two-seater.

Outwardly bumperless, a feature that enhances its sensational lines, the Tuscan bristles with unusual features. There is a two-piece hardtop that transforms the roadster into a coupe and comes apart to be tucked away in the boot when not in use. The rear-window section remains in place.

Then there's the double bonnet which means that when the outer panel is raised, the engine compartment is revealed, completely enclosed, within a second skin. This was created because of the need to provide a smooth transition for air leaving the front-mounted radiator. Although the cover is bolted in place and easily removable, there are simple hatches to provide access to the oil filler and dip stick. Theoretically, there is no need for the Tuscan owner to set eyes on the bespoke straight-six-cylinder engine that lurks beneath.

Neither do the headlamps and rear lights conform to the usual practice. At the front the twin units are deeply recessed into the wings, while the rear lamps are not positioned in the tail but higher up on the back of the roll-over bar, where they can be viewed through the rear window.

With these aspects of the design now to their liking, the Wheeler/McTaggart team decided that perhaps the Six's interior needed re-thinking...The result is a new, luxurious cockpit; its curves are in complete harmony with the leather and aluminium that is used to great effect. Daringly, they have opted for a curved instrument panel, reminiscent of the 1960s, but it comes complete with a state-of-the-art digital read-out.

Since 1994 TVRs have been powered by their own engines. The first of these, conceived by Al Melling's Rochdale-based MCD company, was a V8 used in the Cerbera/Chimaera line. It was followed in 1997 by the appropriately named Straight Six. This was also initially Melling's work but the project was then taken over by TVR's own John Ravenscroft. It is a 4 litre twin-cam unit with the obligatory four valves per cylinder. Drive is conveyed to the rear axle by a five-speed Borg-Warner manual gearbox. Credited with making all the right noises, it is expected to endow this glass fibre-bodied car with a top speed of 185mph (298km/h).

The chassis follows the usual TVR pattern of a robust tubular backbone with similarly strong perimeter frame. It is shorter but similar in execution to its V8-powered Cerbera stablemate.

The Tuscan falls about half way along the TVR range, above the potent V8-engined Griffith and Chimaera roadsters, but below the Cerbera coupes. Production is currently running at 40 cars a week and TVR received some 400 orders for the Speed Six which will now be transferred to the Tuscan. That is assuming the perfectionist Wheeler remains absolutely satisfied with the finished product...

SPECIFICATION	TVR TUSCAN
Engine location	Front, in-line
Configuration	6-cylinder
Bore and stroke	96 x 92mm
Capacity	3996cc
Valve operation	Twin overhead camshafts, 4 valves per cylinder
Horsepower	350bhp @ 6800rpm
Transmission	Five speed
Drive	Rear
Chassis	Multi tubular
Suspension – front	Wishbones and coil springs
Suspension – rear	Wishbones and coil springs
Brakes	Ventilated disc
Top speed	185mph (298km/h)
Acceleration	0-60mph (0-97km/h) 4 seconds

Above: The Tuscan also looks good from the back. Interestingly, the rear window is removable. Note the roll-over bar inside the cabin and chromed tail pipes, about the only brightwork on the car.

Left: The glass-fibre body is bereft of decorative features and relies on its assured form to delight the eye. Under the unique twin-layered bonnet is a 4 litre straight-six engine.

Westfield FW400

The number in this car's name stands for 400 kilograms, that's 882 pounds, and the FW is for Feather Weight. This weight-consciousness helps endow the no-frills sports car with electrifying acceleration and Westfield claim that, on the most powerful version, 60mph (97km/h) arrives in just 3.5 seconds.

Above: The driving compartment is formed as part of the carbon-fibre monocoque, so the fascia, seats and floor are all made of the material.

IN TRUTH the West Midlands-based company says that the road-going two-seater is 'a feather over 400kg' but who's counting? The reality is that this is a design that brings racing car technology to the road.

Launched at the 1998 British Motor Show, it is the work of former Lotus Formula 1 engineer Martin Ogilvie, who has 17 years experience of racing car design.

At the heart of the FW400 is a carbon-fibre-based monocoque structure in an epoxy matrix skin that sandwiches a Nomex honeycomb core and weighs an incredible 110lb (50kg). This extraordinarily rigid structure provides both exceptional strength and safety.

Should this unit suffer accident damage, Westfield make the point that although any repair is a specialist task, it would be limited to the visible area of failure and not be unduly expensive or difficult to undertake.

The weight-saving theme is carried through to the front and rear independent suspension units that have aluminium uprights and hubs which, as a result, weigh about half the usual mass. All-round disc brakes are arrested by aluminium-bodied calipers.

Power comes from Rover's well-proven, 1.8 litre, alloy K Series, twin-overhead unit and this is essentially the 143bhp VVC engine used in the MGF. There is also an alternative 190bhp racing version on offer. Although this is transversely positioned in

Left: The FW400 impressively grips the road, thanks to its soft compound Yokohama Advan tyres. Beneath the rear panel is a Hewland LD200 gearbox; it is located there for optimum weight distribution and ease of access.

Above: British Touring Club Championship driver Robb Gravett in the Westfield; afterwards he declaried: 'This car is sensational... it stops on a postage stamp, accelerates like a rocket ship, speed shifting gear after gear.'

SPECIFICATION	WESTFIELD FW400
Engine location	Front, in line
Configuration	4-cylinder
Bore and stroke	80 x 89mm
Capacity	1796cc
Valve operation	Twin overhead camshafts, 4 valves per cylinder
Horsepower	143bhp @ 7000rpm
Transmission	Five speed
Drive	Rear
Chassis	Advanced composite monocoque
Suspension – front	Wishbones and coil springs
Suspension – rear	Wishbones and coil springs
Brakes	Disc
Top speed	140mph (225km/h)
Acceleration	0-60mph (0-97km/h) 3.5 seconds

the MG, it is mounted in a conventional in-line location in the Westfield. Drive is conveyed by a two-bearing propeller shaft that runs at engine speed to a Hewland five-speed rear transaxle. This is a configuration much favoured by racing car constructors. It gives the FW400 excellent balance that benefits its roadholding.

The design also means that the Hewland is easily accessible, and an optional set of gear ratios can even be fitted if these are required for a specified use.

With weight an ever-present consideration, there are no subframes; major components slot into pre-formed compartments in the hull. The glass-reinforced body consists of three quickly removable sections. Daringly there is no windscreen. Instead there are two wind deflectors, reminiscent of those used on 1930s sports cars, that provide some weather protection for the driver and passenger.

The FW400's interior is equally novel with the dark-coloured carbon fibre very apparent. It is used to form the fascia and seats. The latter are fitted with tailored pads.

Production began in the Spring of 1999 and the company declared that only 30 examples would be built during the year. The 400 is far from being Westfield's only product. It makes the stark two-seater SEiGHT that is powered by a Rover V8 and the Ford-engined 1800. The FW400, by contrast, is by far its most ambitious project to date.

USA: HARNESSING THE HORSEPOWER

 *The sports car is essentially a European creation. It did not arrive in America until after the Second World World, but it was soon to be embraced as a viable concept by General Motors, Ford and Chrysler, the US's Big Three motor manufacturers.*

IN TRUTH it was then that America essentially rediscovered performance motoring because it had produced rugged open two-seaters, like the Mercer Raceabout and Stutz Bearcat, in the years before the First World War. But the breed failed to survive into the 1920s.

These interwar years marked the arrival of the mass-produced sedan. In an era of cheap gasoline, if car makers wanted their products to go faster, they simply enlarged the cubic capacities of their power units. This contrasted markedly with their Old World counterparts who were more intent on increasing performance by improving engine efficiency.

After the Second War, the American public rediscovered the delights of performance motoring, thanks to the MGs and Jaguars from Britain, while Germany and Italy provided two new stars in the respective and distinctive forms of Porsche and Ferrari.

This albeit modest invasion, particularly on the sunny West Coast, soon prompted a response from Detroit, and General Motors was first to throw its stetson into the ring with the Chevrolet Corvette of 1953. The glass-fibre-bodied roadster – the material has featured in every 'Vette since then – was initially powered by a six-cylinder engine, but a V8 arrived in 1955 and this power unit has forever been associated with the model.

Ford followed tentatively with its 'personal' Thunderbird of 1955 but really hit the automotive jackpot in 1964 with the arrival of the sporty Mustang which was aimed foursquare at the post-war baby boomer generation. With 100,000 sold in the first four months following its announcement, it was destined to be one of the fastest-selling cars in the history of the American motor industry. Like the Corvette, the name has proved to be enduring, and the current model commemorates the 35th anniversary of the birth of this fabled model.

Ford V8 power was, in 1962, responsible for transforming the performance of the British AC Ace roadster that was renamed the Cobra. It was the vision of Texan racing driver, Carroll Shelby – he had co-driven the winning DBR1 Aston Martin at Le Mans in '59, and has been deeply involved with the American racing scene ever

since. His Series 1 roadster of 1998, Shelby's first car to be unrelated to any existing model, shows that the old master has lost none of his commitment and enthusiasm for the performance sector.

As engine capacities grew in the booming 1960s, ever more powerful V8s appeared to propel the decade's so-called muscle cars. By the time that Chrysler's Plymouth Superbird Road Runner arrived in 1969, its engine capacity had grown to 7.2 litres and, in racing trim, top speed soared to 220mph (354km/h).

Since the late 1980s the Corporation has wowed visitors to the Detroit Auto Show with a series of sensational concept cars, at least two of which, the Dodge Viper and the Plymouth Prowler, have reached the production line. Perversely, the Dodge is not powered by a V8 engine but a V10 unit. In the world of performance cars, anything is possible!

Left: Anglo-American unity: 1967 AC Cobra 427 Mark III with 7 litre Ford V8.

Above: This 1970 Plymouth Road Runner Superbird Muscle Car used a 7.2 litre V8.

Below: A 1959 Chevrolet Corvette, powered by 4.6 litre V8.

Right: A 1990 Ford Mustang with an original '64 convertible.

Dodge Viper

These days, an increasing number of performance models start life as extravagantly styled concept cars. The Porsche Boxster and Suzuki Cappuccino are cases in point and so is the Dodge Viper.

The Viper's Chrysler-designed but Lamborghini-refined 8 litre V10 pushrod engine.

THIS OUTLANDISH, and rather spartan two-seater roadster appeared at the 1989 Detroit Motor Show. Not only did it proclaim a no-frills, back to basics approach, it also reaffirmed a corporate commitment to the large front engine/rear drive concept. The power unit in question was an 8 litre, cast-iron, V10 pushrod unit, intended to power a new range of Chrysler trucks and sports utilities. This was mounted in a robust tubular-steel chassis with all-independent suspension.

These unconventional mechanicals were concealed beneath an equally unusually styled steel body with fibreglass extremities, utterly distinctive, yet recalling Ferrari and Jaguar styling cues. Another visual ingredient came from the Anglo/America AC

Cobra. Carroll Shelby, its creator, was recruited by Chrysler to provide invaluable input to the development of this concept. The Viper name underlined this relationship.

The public loved the wacky two-seater to the extent that Chrysler decided to put the Viper into production and the first examples began to reach appreciative owners during 1992. Although these outwardly resembled the '89 show car, some changes had taken place beneath the acrylic plastic body. Of these, the most significant concerned the engine: it was extensively reworked by then in-house Lamborghini. Now with an aluminium block, the internal ministrations produced a leap in power from the 300bhp generated by the original to 400bhp. As a result Chrysler

was able to claim a top speed of 165mph (266km/h) with 60 miles an hour (97km/h) arriving in a very respectable 4.5 seconds.

Another of the concept's themes, namely the no-frills approach, was carried through to the production vehicle. The model therefore lacked many of the mechanical and electronic gizmos of the day and thus eschewed four-wheel-drive and anti-lock brakes. The sparsely furnished cockpit further emphasized this approach. There was a fixed rear window and surround reinforced with an integrated roll-over bar in the manner of the Porsche Targa, although a soft top and sidescreens were available as options.

The open car was followed, at the 1993 Detroit show, by a coupe version, and the Viper GTS, as it was called, entered production in 1996. This was a more conventional offering, being better equipped than the roadster with the V10 boosted to 450bhp and performance enhanced by the presence of a front spoiler and rear aerofoil.

Despite its tin top, the GTS weighed less than the open car because of its lighter body and mechanicals. This, coupled with the better aerodynamics of a coupe, made it significantly faster than the original. It could attain 180mph (290km/h).

Further ministrations to the V10 resulted in the Venom roadster with 550bhp on tap, and this in turn paved the way to the even more potent Venom 600 of 1997 with the engine now producing 635bhp. This Viper can sting!

SPECIFICATION	DODGE VIPER GTS
Engine location	Front, in-line
Configuration	V10
Bore and stroke	101 x 98mm
Capacity	7990cc
Valve operation	Pushrod
Horsepower	450bhp @ 5200rpm
Transmission	Six speed
Drive	Rear
Chassis	Tubular steel
Suspension – front	Wishbones and coil springs
Suspension – rear	Wishbones and coil springs
Brakes	Ventilated disc
Top speed	180mph (290km/h)
Acceleration	0-60mph (0-97km/h) 4.2 seconds

Left: The Viper is sold under the Chrysler, rather than Dodge, name in the UK.

Below: The 180mph (290km/h) GTS coupe which is faster than the original roadster.

Chevrolet Corvette

It is, of course, an American legend. The Corvette has been an integral part of the trans-Atlantic performance car scene since 1953. The present version is the sixth generation 'Vette and the magic is still very much in evidence.

The 'Vette coupe was the first body style of the latest generation. The roof panel lifts out for open-air motoring.

INTRODUCED AT the 1997 Detroit Motor Show, it was noticeably shorter than its predecessor because General Motors was looking for European sales. So the traditional American look, with substantial overhangs front and rear, was toned down. Reassuringly, under the bonnet is a big V8. It's a pushrod unit but an aluminium one, and this small block 5.7 litre Chevrolet engine develops a useful 339bhp endowing the car with a top speed of over 170mph (274km/h).

As ever, the chassis is a robust tubular-steel affair with all-round independent suspension and, unusually, transverse leaf springs. They are made of a composite material rather than metal. This is a well-established Corvette feature while the rear-mounted six-speed manual gearbox is inherited from the fifth generation predecessor. The configuration gives it a desirable 50/50 balance to the benefit of its roadholding.

There's a comfortable, well-equipped cockpit but this is strictly a two-seater; the presence of that rear-mounted gearbox precludes space for any additional passengers, however small!

First to appear was the well-established targa-type coupe, with detachable roof panel. It was followed by the now obligatory convertible. Then, for the 1999 season, a third body option was introduced; this is a fixed-head hardtop which revived a 'Vette feature that first appeared back in 1956. Because it lacks the T-bar and additional superstructure of the targa, it is lighter and therefore slightly faster. Even legends have to evolve.

SPECIFICATION	CHEVROLET CORVETTE
Engine location	Front, in-line
Configuration	V8
Bore and stroke	99 x 92mm
Capacity	5666cc
Valve operation	Pushrod
Horsepower	339bhp @ 5400rpm
Transmission	Six speed
Drive	Rear
Chassis	Tubular steel
Suspension – front	Wishbones, transverse leaf spring
Suspension – rear	Wishbones, transverse leaf spring
Brakes	Disc, front ventilated
Top speed	172mph (277km/h)
Acceleration	0-60mph (0-97km/h) 4.7 seconds

Left: Although the Covette is as American as apple pie, the current version outwardly reflects world trends with more than a hint of Ferrari and Honda NSX. The pop-up headlamps have been a feature of the model since the 1963 'Vette Sting Ray.

Ford Mustang

The current Mustang is the latest version of a model that appeared in 1994. Completely redesigned in an era that has seen the increasing popularity of front-wheel drive, the 'Stang remains faithful to the forward engine/rear drive configuration that it inherited from the 1964 original.

Below: The current Mustang is produced in the two body styles shown here. The rear of the convertible (upper) displays what Ford describes as its 'new tri-bar tail lamps'. Also the rear deck is now made from a moulded compound. The coupe version (lower) reveals new chiselled lines with sharper creases, wraparound head lamps and side scoops. A 3.8 litre V6 and 4.6 V8 are available.

P RODUCED IN coupe and convertible forms, with power provided by a 3.8 litre V6, a topline GT coupe was available with a venerable 4.9 litre V8 that gave it a top speed of 137mph (220km/h). It was also used in tuned form in the limited production Cobra version created by Ford's Special Vehicle Team. However this V8 was only briefly employed and it was replaced for the 1996 season by an environmentally cleaner, more fuel-efficient, 4.6 litre single-cam unit that was also available with twin-cam heads.

1999 marks the 35th anniversary of the Mustang's 1964 introduction and the '99 range, that arrived in the Autumn of 1998, were bodily and mechanically enhanced. The galloping pony motif on the radiator grille was once again encircled with a chromed 'corral', just like the original. To underline the anniversary, the model's tri-bar emblem is repeated on the sides of the front wings.

SPECIFICATION	FORD MUSTANG GT
Engine location	Front, in-line
Configuration	V8
Bore and stroke	91 x 91mm
Capacity	4601cc
Valve operation	Single overhead camshaft
Horsepower	260bhp @ 5250rpm
Transmission	Five speed
Drive	Rear
Chassis	Unitary
Suspension – front	MacPherson strut
Suspension – rear	Multi link
Brakes	Disc
Top speed	134mph (216km/h)
Acceleration	0-60mph (0-97km/h) 5.9 seconds

Its lines have been sharpened up, and they not only echo the original car, but also draw on Ford's New Edge styling that, to a greater and lesser extent, is influencing all its models. Wraparound headlamps are also new. More power has been extracted from the engines with the V6 getting an extra 40hp, output rising to 190bhp, while the GT's V8 develops 260bhp. The 305bhp Cobra is a 150mph (241km/h) car.

Thus reinvigorated the Mustang is poised to stampede into the 21st century and beyond. It's called horsepower...

Plymouth Prowler

The Prowler could not have been created anywhere but America. This is because it combines the visual appeal and charisma of that peculiarly trans-Atlantic institution, the hot rod, with the practicality of a road car.

THE PROWLER, like the Dodge Viper featured on pages 86–87, began life as a concept car. In this instance it made its debut at the 1993 Detroit show. The Chrysler Corporation, owner of the populist Plymouth marque, was looking for striking looks to enhance its increasingly dated image.

The purple-hued Prowler certainly drew the crowds. Created by Chrysler's head of design, Tom Gale, a self-confessed hot rodder, the uncompromising two-seater was powered by a 3.5 litre iron V6 with single overhead cams per bank, courtesy of the Chrysler Concorde front-wheel-drive saloon. But the Prowler was a rear-drive model, so its transaxle was transferred to the car's rear, fed via a four-speed automatic gearbox.

Suspension was independent all round and, as befitted its hot rod parentage, the front wishbones were chromed and open to view. The cycle-type front wings were a concession to the practicalities of road running, but the Prowler also catered for its occupants' creature comforts by being fitted with power-assisted steering and twin

Right: The Prowler can be ordered with a matching trailer.

airbags. Unlike Dodge Viper drivers who aren't supposed to mind getting wet, potential Prowler owners were relieved to discover the discreet presence of a power-operated hood.

The public clearly like what it saw, but Chrysler did not give the project the green light until the Autumn of 1994 with production destined to start late in 1997.

The project was allocated to Chrysler's appropriately named 'toy factory' in Conner Avenue, Detroit, which also produces the Viper. Inevitably some of the concept's features have been sacrificed to the realities of quantity production and the demands of everyday motoring. Mostly significantly the aluminium and composite body is longer and wider than the original, and the headlamps, following the contours of the distinctive V-shaped nose, have been enlarged.

Left: There's nothing quite like it! Head-on view of the Prowler with its forged aluminium wishbone independent front suspension and pushrod rocker-arm-operated coil springs much in evidence.

Right: The latest Prowler is powered by an alloy 3.5 litre V6 which replaced a cast-iron unit. Strictly a two-seater, this hot rod for the road was refined with power steering, automatic transmission and electrically operated windows.

In the first year of production just 320 examples were built, but the arrival of the 1998 generation car saw a significant mechanical modification. The original 214bhp V6 powered the 1997 Prowlers, but 1998's models used a new engine, a 3.5 litre V6 that now developed 253bhp which was sufficient to shave one second off the 0 to 60mph (97km/h) figure.

Thus reinvigorated, the Prowler has found appreciative American owners, but it is not available outside the US.

SPECIFICATION	PLYMOUTH PROWLER
Engine location	Front, in-line
Configuration	V6
Bore and stroke	96 x 81mm
Capacity	3518cc
Valve operation	Single overhead camshaft
Horsepower	253bhp @ 6400rpm
Transmission	Four speed automatic
Drive	Rear
Chassis	Bonded and riveted aluminium
Suspension – front	Wishbones and coil springs
Suspension – rear	Multi link and coil springs
Brakes	Disc
Top speed	117mph (188km/h)
Acceleration	0-60mph (0-97km/h) 6.5 seconds

As carrying capacity was limited, particularly with the hood lowered, Chrysler created a purpose-designed trailer which shares the same livery as the car for those owners who want to take their Prowlers on holiday. Manufacture started late in 1997, and initially the car was available in a choice of two body colours, namely purple that echoed the Detroit concept, and a dazzling Prowler yellow of a hue that would put a banana in the shade!

Shelby Series 1

Light weight and turbine-like V8 power are the key ingredients of this car created by Carroll Shelby, father of the AC Cobra. This 170mph (274km/h) open two-seater entered production in 1999, but manufacture is restricted to just 500 examples.

THERE IS a very real difference between the Series 1 and Shelby's previous cars because it is not based on an existing model. The chassis and body have been purpose-designed from the ground up. It was first displayed at the 1997 Los Angles Auto Show. There the silver V8-engined roadster, with its carbon fibre and fibreglass body concealing a square-section tubular-steel chassis, generated considerable public interest. This took place in January, but it was to be another year before the definitive design emerged.

The resulting car – it turns the scales at 2650lb (1202kg) – has an undoubted retro-look with elements of Ferrari and Cobra in

Right: The carbon-fibre and glass-fibre-bodied Shelby two-seater with power provided by a Shelby-enhanced 4 litre Oldsmobile V8.

Below: The bonnet duct permits rapid exit for air that has just passed through the radiator, a proven Shelby feature.

SPECIFICATION	SHELBY SERIES 1
Engine location	Front, in-line
Configuration	V8
Bore and stroke	87 x 84mm
Capacity	3995cc
Valve operation	Twin overhead camshaft, 4 valves per cylinder
Horsepower	320bhp @ 6500rpm
Transmission	Six speed
Drive	Rear
Chassis	Aluminium spaceframe
Suspension – front	Wishbones, rocker-operated coil springs/damper
Suspension – rear	Wishbones, rocker-operated coil springs/damper
Brakes	Ventilated disc
Top speed	170mph (274km/h)
Acceleration	0-60mph (0-97km/h) 4.4 seconds

the mix but it has a distinct and rather European persona of its own. In a quest to save precious pounds, Shelby's engineers have dispensed with the show car's steel chassis and replaced it with an aluminium spaceframe. However, the all-round purpose-designed aluminium wishbone suspension has survived intact.

At the heart of the Shelby is a General Motors 4 litre V8 that comes courtesy of Oldsmobile's luxurious Aurora saloon. Ministrations by Shelby have resulted in output being upped from 250 to some 320bhp, courtesy of new camshafts, improved inlet and exhaust manifolds, and a redesigned, less restrictive exhaust system.

Although the drive in the '97 show car was transferred via a Richmond six-speed gearbox attached directly to the engine, in the production car this was replaced by a rear-mounted RBT/ZF transaxle. It receives power via a torque tube that also plays a structural role. The robust gearbox has a competition lineage that reaches back to the 1960s vintage Le Mans-winning Ford GT40, a project with which Shelby was much involved.

The formative '97 Series 1 had a rather stark cockpit, but marketing considerations – the production car retails at $108,000 (£67,500) – meant a re-think in that department. Although retro elements abound, it is now fitted with air conditioning, electric windows and a radio and CD player. However, this a strictly two-person car. Driver and passenger can never ignore Carroll Shelby's racing roots because, like any competition car, the Series 1 has no boot and, as a result, there's no room to store a spare wheel.

It is built at Shelby American's new manufacturing facility located in the grounds of the Las Vegas Speedway, and a day's tuition there is included in the purchase price. Buyers normally collect their cars from the factory, although they are being marketed by 25 selected Oldsmobile/Team Shelby dealers.

And if their 76-year-old creator is right, many Series 1s will find their way on to the race track. If pedigree is anything to go by, that's where they belong.

THEY ALSO RAN

One of the more fascinating aspects of the performance car world is that it is never static! Car makers, both large and small, continue to produce designs of style and ingenuity for an expanding market sector which is looking for something a little different from the norm. These are just a few of them.

Caterham 21

IN 1973 Caterham Cars of Coulsdon, Surrey, which had held the sole concession for Lotus's stark and long-lived Seven since 1967, took over its manufacture and the outcome was the revised Caterham Seven that endures in Super Seven guise to this day. Refined and uprated over the years, it is currently powered by Rover's K Series engine and some 8000 have been produced. In 1994 Caterham took the Seven concept one step further with the introduction of the 21. This, in essence, takes the Seven's mechanicals but uses a wider chassis, clad with a new all-enveloping fibreglass body.

More aerodynamically efficient, and available in 1.6 and 1.8 litre forms, with a top speed of about 125mph (201km/h), the 21 is notably faster than its square-rigged progenitor. But with the topline 1.8 litre VVC version selling for £28,500, it is some £5000 more expensive than the Seven. Ironically, Lotus now produces the Elise, a spiritual successor of the Seven, which undercuts them both.

Ginetta G4

THIS IS a car that refused to die. The G4 was introduced in 1961 with a tubular chassis and coil springing, independent at the front, a Ford Anglia engine and an open fibreglass body. The attractive two-seater sports racer, that could also be legally driven on the road, survived until 1968 by which time some 390 had been built. But 13 years later, in 1981, the company reintroduced it in revamped Mark IV form.

Left: The Caterham 21 with Rover K Series power and currently available in potent 1.8 litre VVC (variable valve control) form.

Above right: Ginetta G4 Zetec, available in roadster and coupe forms, combines Jaguar E-Type-inspired styling with Ford's modern 1.8 litre twin cam.

Right: The Lea-Francis 30/230 at the 1998 British Motor Show. This traditional roadster is based on a modern stamped and bonded aluminium frame.

However, Ginetta was sold in 1989, and later, in 1992, the rights to the G4 and the mid-engined G12 were acquired by Tamotsu Maeda, its Japanese importers. It, in turn, commissioned Dare UK, run by the Walklett brothers who had founded Ginetta, to manufacture it for them (see pages 66–67) at its factory at Colchester, Essex. Now revised as the Ginetta G4 Zetec and mostly exported to Japan, as its name indicates it is still Ford-powered but now the powerplant is a 1.8 litre Zetec twin-cam four-cylinder engine.

Lea-Francis 30/230

THE COVENTRY-based bicycle-maker Lea and Francis began building cars in 1903. After a sometimes financially turbulent history it was bought in 1962 by businessman-cum-enthusiast Barrie Price. The latest model, the 30/230, an open two-seater, made its debut at the 1998 British Motor Show. One of Price's partners in the venture is Jaguar's former director of product engineering, Jim Randle.

He had overall responsibility for the Jaguar XJ6 saloon of 1986, and he has designed the new Leaf's aluminium chassis and active suspension. With power courtesy of a 3 litre V6 Vauxhall engine, the 155mph (249km/h) car is to be built by Tim Paine's Park Sheet Metal in Coventry. He is the other partner in the revival of the oldest British-owned car company. Production is scheduled to start in the year 2000.

Strathcarron SC

THE STRATHCARRON, a new British race and road car, is due to enter production in 1999. Based on a concept vehicle conceived by Izusu and General Motors engineer Simon Cox, it is built around a composite monocoque hull. The aluminium body is produced by the Dutch Hoogovens company while the engine, unusually, is a Triumph 1.2 litre four-cylinder motorcycle unit. It drives the car's rear wheels via a six-speed sequential gearbox.

The Strathcarron company specializes in pre-production development work for the motor industry, and its technical director is Colin Spooner, formerly of Lotus. The intention is to manufacture separate road- and race-going versions of the design; the former has a projected top speed of 125mph (201km/h). It is hoped that the car will sell for under £20,000.

And finally, Volkswagen's WR12 engine

WHEN VOLKSWAGEN unveiled a mid-engined W12 supercar at the 1997 Tokyo motor show, it was widely predicted that this coupe would spearhead a challenge to VW's Mercedes-Benz rival at the 1999 Le Mans 24 hour race. At its heart was VW's new compact WR12, a 5.8 litre 414bhp engine created by combining two existing 2.8 litre VR6 units. The 48-valve V12 could also be used in a new generation of luxury saloons to challenge the Mercedes S-class. In 1998 an expansive Volkswagen, headed by the dynamic Ferdinand Piech, emerged victorious in the battle for Rolls-Royce motor cars, although, at the time of writing, it has forfeited the make to BMW and retained Bentley.
The first fruits of this liaison came in 1999 with the arrival of the mid-engined Bentley Hunaudières concept coupe (see page 64) powered by a V16 version of the versatile WR.

In 1998 VW also bought the moribund Bugatti marque and it displayed the big EB112 concept four-seater coupe at the 1998 Paris motor show. Now Volkswagen has two more sporting makes which can be powered by the versatile WR12, road cars are under development and Le Mans beckons. Both marques have already won the event, Bentley in 1924 and 1927–31 and Bugatti in 1937 and 1939. And Piech, grandson of Ferdinand Porsche, who once worked for the family firm, was the creator of the mighty 917 that gave Porsche its first victory there in 1970...

Index